All You Need is A.S.K (Attitude-Skills- Knowledge)

How Attitude, Skills, and Knowledge Drive Sales Success

"A.S.K, The Best Thing To Reach Your Goals In Life…"

By

TALEB HAMMAD

iUniverse books may be ordered through booksellers or by contacting:

iUniverse
1663 Liberty Drive
Bloomington, IN 47403
www.iuniverse.com
1-800-Authors (1-800-288-4677)

Because of the dynamic nature of the Internet, any web addresses or links contained in this book may have changed since publication and may no longer be valid. The views expressed in this work are solely those of the author and do not necessarily reflect the views of the publisher, and the publisher hereby disclaims any responsibility for them.

Any people depicted in stock imagery provided by Thinkstock are models, and such images are being used for illustrative purposes only.
Certain stock imagery © Thinkstock.

ISBN: 978-1-5320-3897-6 (sc)
ISBN: 978-1-5320-3898-3 (e)

Library of Congress Control Number: 2017918785

Print information available on the last page.

iUniverse rev. date: 01/04/2018

Publication Details

About the Author

Coming from a corporate background Taleb successfully worked in business development projects for various startup companies, Taleb is a certified trainer, he is also certified in Human Resource, he delivered training courses in soft skills. He has helped clients in several industries and sectors such as Retail, Pharmaceutical, FMCG and Human Resource, up-skill their teams and achieves better return of expectations-ROE. Taleb holds a B.Sc in Pharmaceutical Science, he is a fellow member of Institute of Leadership and Management and a member of American Society of Training and Development. Taleb has spent 21 years working for USA largest pharmaceutical corporates. He developed, trained and motivated thousands of sales and marketing managers. He received several awards for exceptional achievements as a General Manager and learning and Development Manager. Taleb delivers a variety of skill development workshops focusing on negotiation, management, and leadership. Currently, he is working as an Executive Director for a high-end healthcare facility in New York dealing with marketing, social media, and customer satisfaction. He has attended as speaker conferences, talk shows and was interviewed in business books.

Dedication

Making sense of the fast-paced world around us, what to do when you are in the midst of making a decision and need more info to decide, fine-tuning your skills for better consistent achievement every single time in your career and personal life, this is dedicated to you, wondering minds that just want to be the best.

Acknowledgement

Throughout the process of writing this book, many family members and friends influenced me and helped me out, thank you. I'd also like to give special thanks to the all my trainees for their active participating and feedback and contributions that made this book as practical as possible as it is.

Contents

Preface

Attitude, Skills and Knowledge are the three main pillars of success. You need to have the right attitude around people, and with clients and your employees, you should have the right knowledge on how you should achieve your goals, how to plan them and what your industry and target audience is, and skills that are needed to do all this. Presenting your product or service is a key issue for any company that wants to sell and do business. The most important thing about a good presentation is to create interest and show that you are not like others, that you have something special, that your client or prospect has a problem that you can solve. This book emphasizes on the selling factors and selling pitch. It helps the salesperson to boost up company revenue by polishing up their skills. This book answers about sales management by sharpening up your skills and talents. If you have the right attitude and the skills that you need to accomplish all your goals in life.

Chapter 1

Sharpen Skills Fine Tunes Your Results

"There's no lotion or potion that will make sales faster and
easier for you - unless your potion is hard work."
- Jeffrey Gitomer

Believe it or not, from birth until we die, we are always selling something to someone, regardless of whether we are teachers, doctors, lawyers or parents. Just as a mother needs to sell certain values to her children to be a good person, the teacher, the surgeon, or the judge need to sell their best to achieve success. That is achieved with the help of other people, whom we must influence or persuade to create and decide for us, whether to get a job or just networking for friends. Regardless of the brand, product or service, if the seller fails to sell first, and fails to connect with the customer, it is going to be very difficult to sell. Sales executives are much more than just a salesperson. This is an independent position that pursues the maximum number of sales, is also related to professional specialization.

Professionalism, in effect, is a distinctive feature of the sales executive. Both, regarding its preparation and its specialization and constant training, seeks to combine the increase in sales and the pursuit of customer satisfaction with them. That is to say, on the one hand, the realization of the sale supposes the end of the operation, but only if the client sees his expectations fulfilled he will not return it nor, in case, will ask for some discount. Likewise, if the purchase did not satisfy you will probably not buy again . Therefore, the sales executive establishes a longer-term relationship with the customer, seeking satisfaction and fidelity. A great challenge, no doubt, that only professionalization can face.

The technical knowledge, about the product or service, are highly valued among the sellers of any sector. However, different skills represent a real added value for sales professionals. What are these skills? What competitions are the most precious in the world of sales? What about the natural talent for sale? There is no doubt that not everyone has the same predisposition and ease to perform the difficult sales activity. Selling is an art, but it also requires certain skills that can be learned or trained. In fact, only when we have the necessary skills only then can we become the best salesmen. That is why being a good sales executive is a very well-paid position.

Likewise, many people are also looking for ways to become good salespeople, but few succeed. Here are some skills that every sales executive should have to advance his career:

Knowing how to listen and knowing how to speak: Being willing to listen and doing so by demonstrating empathy with the prospective buyer also implies knowing how to speak. Do it using a selected vocabulary, adapting to the communicative style of the interlocutor and demonstrating the ease of speech. The ability to listen, a good presence, be empathetic and enthusiastic are points in favor that add to the time to incite the purchase. In short, it is a question of taking the buyer to his land, making him believe otherwise.

Equal people, balanced personality, and integrity bring good feelings that provoke positive attitudes. Among other aspects, potential buyers will appreciate honesty and loyalty to the company as values that convey reliability. Taking work as a duty, being organized and living it also as a motivating activity translates into a significant advantage when it comes to getting more sales. This implies from the way of approaching the day to day to the way of presenting itself or the accomplishment of formative activities. A good salesman should know how to see the opportunities and hunt them on the fly. Having the gift of opportunity, being in the right place at the right time is another way to be a professional. Moreover, by the way, always ends up giving deserved rewards.

It is essential for a salesperson to demonstrate excellent communication skills. It is necessary to transmit messages so that the customers understand, reliably, what the seller intends to communicate, regarding the product or service it sells. The good salesman anticipates, with initiative and energy, in his relationship with the customer and in his main objective, which is the closure of sales. This extends to key issues such as offering new discounts, or alternative products or services, seeking, if possible, new customer needs. In the world of sales, people with a high tolerance for frustration and, above all, persevering and insistent. It is customary among marketers who show exceptional ability to create a good bond with the customer but do not demonstrate the interest necessary to close a sale effectively.

In addition to the relationship with the customer, the salesperson has to demonstrate a high capacity to manage his/her agenda and all the documentation related to visits, reports, etc. This is one of the most sought-after skills among good sellers since it is prevalent for them to lack it. Learning to communicate in a correct, clear and precise manner is an indispensable skill for our professional life, and more so if it is someone who is in the sales area in a micro, small or medium-sized company because their effective participation can make a difference in the business. Regardless of the industry to which the SME is focused, the vendor with communication skills will be able to relate better to customers and allow them to attract new ones. It will also help you solve problems, make your ideas better known and project a good professional image.

Here are some recommendations to improve your communication skills:

- **Make eye contact**
  Seeing a person in the eye is the best way to convey trust. In this way, we can let our clients know that we are interested in what he says and that we are listening attentively.

- **Gesturing**
  Specialists point out that 90% of communication is non-verbal. That is, our body movements communicate more than we believe. That is why we must observe and practice since a gesture can persuade, convince and create trust more than an elaborate speech.

- **Get to the point**
  Having mastery of our communication does not translate into talking a lot, making endless presentations or sending mileage emails. The recommendation to convey our messages efficiently and accurately is to focus on being clear in our ideas and eliminating the filling.

- **Listen**
  If you are willing to be a good communicator, you have to be a good listener. The person who knows how to listen does not lose information, asks appropriate questions and understands his interlocutor. Learn to listen to the customer to meet your needs.

- **Ask**
  One of the communication problems presented by companies is a misunderstanding. Sometimes we avoid asking questions for fear of ridicule, however, being able to openly express doubts and admit when we do not understand an idea allows us to achieve a better understanding.

- **Read**
  Having the habit of reading on a regular basis offers us multiple benefits such as improving our oral and written communication, better spelling and expanding our vocabulary. Reading news and relevant information from your industry will also provide interesting conversation topics to establish contacts and meet potential customers.

- **Choose the correct channels**
  Is your communication medium always the email? You could get much more if you get close to talking personally with some clients. Sometimes a phone call can

be more personal and efficient than an email. Use your perception to identify which channel is most convenient for each client.

- **Be professional**
  Using casual language with your colleagues is fine. However, it is important to identify the times when your language should be formal.

- **Do not interrupt**
  Avoid completing other people's speech with your own ideas or divert the subject from a conversation. It allows people to communicate their thoughts without interruption and then express their doubts or comments.

Applying these recommendations in your interaction with clients will allow you to establish a better connection and create a channel of communication and trust with them. Put them into practice and see how they will help you project a good image, as well as position your SME in the market and attract new customers, which translates into profit, prestige, and growth.

What Is More Important: The Brand, The Product Or The Seller?

Studies say people buy people first; then the brand and finally the product. In a consultative sale, 75% of the purchase decision is determined by the seller's trust to the customer; while the remaining 25% is defined by the mark (18%) and the product (7%). Here we realize the importance, importance, of the seller in the sale, despite having with him a product or a brand of much trajectories, of great value. That is why we say people buy people. In a very high percentage of unsuccessful sales, salesperson is responsible. However, if I review the statistics and see the importance of my action, my personal brand, I become more responsible, that does not mean that I will win all sales, but I will learn from each one of them. One should always pay more for a product, people do not always buy cheaper products.

What to Do When the Price of A Product Or Service Is Very Expensive?

When a customer says that the product is too expensive, he is not saying it because the person is a miser, he is saying it because the seller has not given him the reason why I should pay more for a product, people do not always buy cheaper, and that's a lie. If it were so in this country would not see so many Porsche, Ferrari, and BMW. That tells us that there are salesmen who have been able to show the buyer why they should pay that difference. In business relationships convincing is an imperative, being attractive to our customers is not something that should be negotiated, either you are, or you are obsolete. The science of persuasion in the sale is a field that I am passionate because when the companies internalize, it improves their commercial results.

There is a power to capture the public, influence the undecided and motivate the purchase. It is not a question of any magical knowledge but a scientific one. The science of persuasion comes from social psychology. Persuasion is something scientific, that works and can be demonstrated with real numbers and cases. Too much research has been done on this subject. Generating the feeling of credibility and trust in a customer is something that can be measured and inexorably increases your sales. When speaking of influence and persuasion, it is important that we write down the idea behind what you sell there is an ethical end. Otherwise, things will not go very well. If by persuasion techniques you dedicate to make the life of others worse, you will not end up very well.

The main problem with some people is that they know the technique, but they do not have the attitude. Therefore they generate incoherence when talking with their clients. The problem with other people is that they have the right attitude, but they do not know the technique, and therefore they lose so many opportunities. For me, the science of persuasion in selling lies in having an excellent attitude (win-win) and a refined technique like that of Roger Federer when he jumps onto the track, which does not seem to be dishevelled throughout the game. After much practice selling you will end up having mastery, and that means having control of the situation at almost every moment.

In short, the science of persuasion studies the factors that make us say "yes." That is why we are so interested in studying it in commercial relations because it offers us many keys to increase our influence. In particular, we are going to see some principles:

The principle of reciprocity. This principle tells us that when you do a favor (pay debts and treat others as we are treated) to someone, that person usually feels obliged to return the favor. Think about how many tricks you can apply using this principle:

Give Something To Your Clients

So if you give something of value to your prospects and make sure it is personalized, you will receive a return from them. For example, if you have a blog where you offer valuable information to your readers for free and helps make your life better, your visitors are much more likely to feel compelled to buy something from your website.

Coherence and Commitment

If you get your prospects will commit to something relatively small and usually at no cost, such as downloading a report, you are increasing the likelihood of them becoming your customers. That is because we all tend to appear coherent in front of the others and, therefore, to be consistent with what we have said or done. Moreover, once we have publicly committed to something or someone, we are much more likely to fulfil that commitment.

Approval

Usually, people are influenced by the actions of other people, and we look at what most people think or do to determine what is right. For example, if we observe that a particular restaurant is always crowded, we are more likely to give it a try. So to show our prospects the testimonies of our satisfied customers are fundamental to achieve the action we want.

Sympathy

People are more likely to follow the people we like, either because they are close to or like us, because they make us feel good or because they simply wake us up. It is what is known in English as Like-ability. When someone we love and respect recommends something in particular, such as a book, we tend to pay attention. So take advantage of that in your favor and use your web page (especially the section "About Us"), social networks and other communication channels to spread your ideas and arouse sympathy.

Authority

People follow the advice of experts for the credibility they offer. So try to create authority and show credibility, and your sales will increase. When you believe that something ends, you increase your need and desire to have it. And that is one of your best weapons to persuade your future clients.

Basically, product or service is more attractive when its availability is limited or when we feel we lose the opportunity to buy it under favorable conditions (either a product with limited units or a special offer about to expire). Keep that in mind, apply it consistently, and you will be able to see the changes in a short period of time. As you can see, it is not enough to tell people what they achieve if they are buying your product or service, you need to awaken their desires, create affinity, convince them that it is just what they need and give them plenty of reasons to identify with you and why they should be your customers.

> "Sales are contingent upon the attitude of the
> salesman - not the attitude of the prospect."
> - W. Clement Stone

Selling is taking the time and care to find out what a person really needs and then finding solutions to that need. Many sellers start to be very successful, they know how to speak well, and they start to add impressive sales closures during their first few months, but then, without them understanding what's going on, their sales start to fall. They no longer cared about the customer, they did not care to continue to serve him. Remember that it will always be easier to keep a satisfied customer than to get new ones. Beware of the service, beware of neglecting the customers, careful to consider them a number in the statistics nothing more.

Always remember that "It is not personal." The main factor of discouragement in a seller is rejection; nobody likes it. That is why it is imperative that you understand that the problem is not the objection of a potential customer what matters, but your emotional reaction to that objection. If you manage to keep your mind cold to any rejection or criticism, you can handle it without any problem.

You must develop the ability to be calm and calm; the ability to identify the emotions of your prospects; and you must learn that behind every objection there can always be a benefit. "Yeah, just like you read it." Learning to interpret emotions through body language can be useful "from diplomacy and police to nursing and psychotherapy." Sales are no exception, an efficient use of body language can help us close a deal. Here are some elements that can help any individual to reach an agreement or make a sale:

Always Smile: The Positive Reaches Of A Smile Are Enormous.

"Smiles have an advantage over all other emotional expressions: the human brain prefers happy faces, recognizes them more quickly and quickly than those with negative expressions, a known effect of the "advantage of the happy face."
- Daniel Goleman

With a good smile, you will provoke a good predisposition in the client to listen to you. Remember; a sincere smile is characterized: "by the involuntary activation of two muscle groups," there is elevation at both corners of the mouth, symmetrically and the second group, wrinkles at the corners of the eyes (crow's feet). Always greet your customers. In doing so, veil directly into the eyes - while you smile - and offer your palm upward, the preceding will project security and helpfulness. Those who offer their hand in this way are persons inclined to assist others or to establish constructive forms of competition.

Take care that your greeting is firm, comfortable and full contact; it is also important that your hand is dry. A sweaty salute, giving the hollowed hand, partial (fingers only) or "warm" generates mistrust and an image of insecurity. Your posture should be open at all times, folding your arms, putting a folder or a bundle of fingers on your chest will create a barrier of communication, making it harder to communicate efficiently and generate empathy with your client.

On the other hand, tilting your head and slightly tilting the body trunk forward, will help you generate understanding, empathy, and closeness with your client. From 1.2 to 2 meters is a good distance to negotiate a sale. Being closer can generate discomfort and further disinterest. Self-manipulations or manipulators consist of touching the face, hair or ears with hands. Also includes, "Rubbing the nose; remove lint, real or imaginary threads of clothing; shaking off dust or dandruff; adjusting glasses; play with the hair; stretch, caress or twist necklaces, earrings or jewellery. These gestures allow us to know the state of alteration (nervousness, worry, anguish, discomfort, insecurity, annoyance, etc.) of an individual at a given moment. In a sale, it is as if our body language digests, "Nor do I believe what I am saying. "Use illustrators when you talk about the advantages of your product or service: Illustrators give the impression that the subject is being talked about and are signs of honesty.

Take Care of your Image

"When an individual comes to the presence of others, they usually try to acquire information about him or to put into play what they already have. They will be interested in their general socio-economic status, their concept of themselves, their attitude towards them, their competence, their integrity, etc."
- Erving Goffman

The above sentence illustrates the importance of the first impression; it can simply be final. So we must carefully look at the details of our image, a loose collar button, an ill-fitting tie, a sloppy knot, dishevelled, dull shoes, a spotted spot on the face or yellow teeth, among many other details, can generate an image of lack of professionalism. Customers will distrust you immediately. Always try to control that first impression that you take away from you. The seller's attitude to success. For many, the seller's capabilities are something innate that comes along with the personality of the person himself. It is true that you have to have certain skills to be a good salesperson, but it also requires a hard job for which you must put your best attitude. Showing honesty, trust in the product, organization and, above all, leadership are qualities that must be present, and that cannot be ignored in the figure of the seller.

A Successful Salesperson

A salesperson must convey trust, so it is of no avail if his attitude is lacking in honesty and integrity. It is true that you can get a sale with little lies, but you only get that: a sale. A seller should not settle for the sale, what you should always look for is to generate a network of contacts through a first consumer. Something that will be much easier if you use honesty instead of a little lie. A good salesperson will never think of selling a heater in the desert or ice to Inuits. Even if he could cajole them with a pious lie, he knows that in the long run, that lie can bring dire consequences. Undoubtedly, something that deserves to invest our time as salespeople is to know what customers need and create a relationship of trust with them. When you are approached, you have to make them see that what you are looking for is that they take the best product for them. It is not about looking like you care about consumers; you really should want to help your customers.

In this regard, some may wonder why we waste our time on this instead of taking advantage of it to look for more sales. The answer is simple. At the time of purchase, consumers are guided by their emotions. Making a sale is "easy," but repeating is more complex. We do not want consumers of a single purchase; we want to make them loyal and to choose our products whenever they need them. For this, personal relationships, face-to-face marketing is what works best since the beginning of the sales office. Closely linked to the previous point and the generation of confidence towards the consumer, we would find this statement:

A seller must always believe that the product or service with which he works has a great value for the customer to whom it is offered.

The chances that your product has a better reception among potential customers are greater if you trust its benefits, not only as a seller but also as a potential consumer. We must find that point, that difference that makes the product so good and identifies why we would buy it ourselves. If you do not believe in what you are selling, customers will notice it and, even if you do not want to, you will get insecure about what is being offered.

Organization and control of timing. In the training of vendors and hostesses, they spend much time teaching them how to organize and orient their calendars to arrange business visits, meet clients, offer products or other.

However, **does this really influence sales?** Yes, and it will also be noticed on several fronts.

In the business world, there are certain expectations about the organization and those that do not appear to be, are perceived as less professional although it is not so. In reality, how well or poorly organized a schedule will influence the way you act when selling. The real usefulness of these schedules and this organization is that the seller is able to identify the perfect moment in which the consumers are predisposed to the purchase, or that such important customer is ready to close a deal. Behind this is a lot of work, hours of studying the market and patterns of behavior, but, all this effort is rewarded if we are at the perfect time for the transaction to take place. Being there, at that moment, is only achieved by being a well-organized salesman with a working system that works. One of the phrases that most listeners sell is something like;

*"NO, you already have it, with or without trying. So
we will have to see if YES is achieved."*

Moreover, that is NOT going to be present from the first moment, but it can be changed! The most important thing to overcome is not to be afraid of it. Since rejection is when we can learn more or redirect our strategy. Because of the time is not the time to be creative and look for alternatives to offer the products.

Leadership Attitude

What is leadership attitude? To answer, we turn to a phrase from former President Dwight Eisenhower that defined it as:

*"The art of getting someone to do something you
want to do because he wants to do it."*

Moreover, how is it achieved? Leadership, like most skills, is something you do not have innately, but you have to work it out. Security and trust are vital if you are to develop that leadership role, which is so much needed to be a successful salesperson.

If you want to achieve that security and confidence to achieve the maximum benefit in the field of sales, it will be necessary to study and to know in depth:

- To ourselves, our product and our company
- The market, the competition and the variations that exist
- Customers and final consumers and their needs

When a salesperson is able to know these areas in depth, he already has enough capacity to acquire the leadership of a project with total security and confidence in what he is doing. A leader-minded salesperson will know how to handle customers so that, as Eisenhower said, do what you want to do because they want to do it. For example, a car salesman trying to sell you a specific car. Your mission is that you do not perceive that desire for sale on your part, but that you are the one who thinks you want to buy that car and not the one you brought home. To do so will convince you that it is best for you, in fact, if you are a good seller you are surely right, and that car is better for you than the one you had in mind.

Sales should never be to pressure someone to buy a product they do not need. When you have a good product, for example, a good car, it is easy to recommend it and convey that enthusiasm when it comes to sales. The professional seller should know how to do the same when the product or service is not so good. Incorporating honesty, integrity, and ethics into your transactions leads to a good relationship with your customers, which means that they themselves will be the ones that will generate new business opportunities.

Chapter 2

The Power of a Well-Communicated Message

"The art of communication is the language of leadership."
- James Humes

The man in his need to communicate has been faced with overcoming distances to be able to express his ideas and thoughts, to achieve this he began to use his media. Throughout the history of humanity, man has created various forms of communication, which have been very useful for its development personal and social. Thanks to the technological advances, it has been possible to count on systems of more efficient communications, of greater scope and of greater power, which has allowed us to reach impressive technologies to which we have access daily. It is important to mention that communication has a special application in the business field since it is central to the culture and organizational climate that have a significant influence on the specification of values and beliefs organizations that together help achieve the main objective that the organization pursues.

In the process of communication, since the intention to transmit some message is generated until the receiver interprets that message, there are many important stages for that communication to be effective. One of them is to know how to correctly transmit the message and use a language that is commonly accepted by those involved in the process if not, it is possible that what is intended to communicate has nothing to do with what the receiver interprets. Applied to our work: it is imperative that we do not use a technical language when we are trying to inform a user. Techniques and expressions that are not adequate to the level of understanding of the receiver can lead to mistakes or misinterpretations that can sometimes be irreversible or difficult to remedy (and taking into account our scope of work).

According to McCaskey, MB (1979) managers can improve their understanding of communication between people by managing images, scenarios, and body language. If a manager in an organization talks about making an "end of a career," what is he trying to say? Do you see the life of the organization as a game? Do you see a risk or are you nominating yourself for a role of the hero? Or is he just saying that anyway he goes with a project, regardless? The truth is that we cannot know what he is saying. It is too easy to interpret the metaphors that others employ to accommodate our meanings but ignore the fact that metaphors have idiosyncratic meanings that should be heard. McCaskey describes three ways managers convey messages about themselves and the way they see the world. He exhorts to see these forms - their metaphors, their office settings, their tone and their body language that accompanies their speech - in the form of communication. Like speech or mathematics, these are languages that can be learned. With their skill, a manager can see and can hear what is really happening when people talk, what hidden messages they are sending all the time.

McCaskey gives some tips on what to see and hear when trying to understand others, but be careful with simplistic interpretations as all messages occur in a context. His tone and his body language that accompanies his speech - by way of communication. Like speech or mathematics, these are languages that can be learned. With their skill, a manager can see and can hear what is happening when people talk, what hidden messages they are sending all the time. McCaskey gives some tips on what to see and hear when trying to understand others, but be careful with simplistic interpretations as all messages occur in a context.

"Take advantage of every opportunity to practice your communication skills so that when important occasions arise, you will have the gift, the style, the sharpness, the clarity, and the emotions to affect other people."

- Jim Rohn

His tone and his body language that accompanies his speech - by way of communication. Like speech or mathematics, these are languages that can be learned. With their skill, a manager can see and can hear what is really happening when people talk, what hidden messages they are sending all the time. McCaskey gives some tips on what to see and hear when trying to understand others, but be careful with simplistic interpretations as all messages occur in a context. For example, if we find that our people are not doing what we want them to do, the error can be ours, says Klain, G. (2000). It seems simple for leaders to agree that their subordinates do what they are asked to do, but research shows that it is not so simple. Sometimes leaders only give action orders without explaining why. And other times they do not strive to show their intentions in a clear way. Why do not people follow simple instructions? Sometimes it seems like sharing is silly. It could be called insubordination, or lack of motivation. Perhaps there are great organizational barriers that we need to clarify. It is not difficult to find all kinds of problems in the company and the employees. Klein and his colleagues have studied business and military leaders for many years.

Message Interpretation

"Communication - the human connection - is the key to personal and career success."

- Paul J. Meyer

The importance of a perfect understanding of the meaning of the message transmitted to the participants in the formation is fundamental for the success of the same. In the communication we use in a training event, there are a number of extremely important factors that should be taken care of in detail to ensure that the message is understood, reaches the interlocutor and is useful for his work. It is evident that it is not only a matter of content, although it is a fundamental aspect, but also of form. For this reason, the use of verbal, verbal and non-verbal language must be consistent and consistent and be aligned with the intended message. However, sometimes the possible interpretations that the different groups participating in the training can give the same message, especially when the group presents a marked heterogeneity, are sometimes not addressed or envisaged. Undoubtedly, variables such as level of training, previous experience in the area, personal and professional situation and mood are "conditions" that facilitate the filtering of information and guide the interpretation of meaning to a particular place according to criteria that often seem difficult to understand.

But is it important for the consultant to anticipate the different interpretations that his message can bring about according to which contexts? Or put another way should the consequences and impact of the consultant's message be foreseen? Should we anticipate answers to overcome potential resistance? Test development competencies. It is often a challenge that a good consultant-trainer must undertake and work with dedication to adapt to the different situations that happen. On the other hand, it is a pre-adaptation exercise aimed at ensuring the intended competence development with training. Otherwise, training, at least for some group, will not make sense. Therefore, not only a high level of communication competence is sufficient, understanding it as the capacity to adapt the message to the level of understanding and linguistic training of the interlocutors, guaranteeing the attention and facilitating the understanding, but the foresight and pre-adaptation to the interpretation of the message that the participants will make up as a more important component.

This is a field that cultivates Pragmatics or Linguistic Pragma, an area linked to the importance that the context gives rise to in interpreting the meaning that has to do with the situation, that is, with everything that surrounds the speakers and conforms their way of understanding the world and the things that surround it.

A communicative situation comes to my mind where the interpretation of the message was extremely disparate depending on the place from which the listener interpreted the meaning. Curiously, where one group only saw advantages, the other only perceived inconveniences. Why?

In an environment of continuous improvement and developing a training-awareness in the optimization of production processes, efficiency and productivity, managers or organizational area understood the message as the road to move to the sustainability of your company.

Team training, on the contrary, the operating line feared a potential imbalance in its workload, a worsening of the technical conditions related to its day-to-day and who knows if future depreciation of certain functions, due to the increase in the speed of the process, the grouping jobs and increasing the productivity of the workforce. The real task of the organization, in this case, is to make lean its production process to increase its responsiveness and to be able to serve the market in better conditions by establishing optimal service agreements. Nothing could be further from the dreaded amortization of posts and the increase in labor fatigue through exorbitant increases in the workload (which would put the quality down). That real purpose understood in a clairvoyant way by some participants according to their interpretation of things and provoking misgivings for others, must be transmitted in such a way that all share the same message and are aligned in the same direction.

The Right Way to Communicate

"Wise men speak because they have something to say;
Fools because they have to say something."

- Plato

One of the elements that people use as the main tool to interact or interrelate with our peers is communication, as it is used for both sending and receiving information. Communication is a fairly broad topic that manages several characteristics, types, and elements that constitute it, so in this article, we will talk about some important things about this topic. It is common that in our day to day, during a habitual communication with our parents, friends, and companions and other people with whom we interact, we are not accustomed to handling and to practice a communication of effective form that helps us to be able to transmit and to receive the messages correctly. The question that now arises is, what can be called effective communication? The communication starts from the principle that for the exchange of information there must be an issuer (who transmits the information) and a receiver (who receives the information).

The sender when sending the information must know how to choose the appropriate communication channel so that the receiver can receive and, above all, understand the message that is being transmitted. When you receive the message, you must understand, interpret and send a response (also known as feedback), thus producing a conversation or an exchange of information between them. Once the correct communication channel has been chosen, it is necessary for the sender to ensure that the receiver understands the information so that all interaction between the two can be made on the same basis. It is also necessary that the information can be transmitted at the time that is appropriate, that is to say at the time that is needed, and to whoever needs it.

It is believed that who is a good speaker, knows how to expose or give a good speech is applying effective communication. Since it is thought that we communicate correctly is to know how to transmit the information we want, but the truth is that to handle good communication, this must be back and forth, that means that it is composed of two fundamental parts: knowing how to speak and how to listen.

Emphasis is placed on speaking skills to know how to give a good speech or to make a good presentation. However, in spite of being very important, these are only oriented to know how to transmit a message to an audience or public, that is to say, it is a unidirectional communication. But very little importance is given to the ability to know how to listen. The ability to listen to the message we receive is called Active Listening. As its name suggests, this ability is to know how to listen to the information they send us actively. To know how to listen is not only to receive the message that they send us, it also implies being able to understand it, to interpret it correctly and above all to be able to watch closely the person who transmits it so that they are attentive to their gestures, gestures, and movements.

There are many things and elements around us that can cause us distractions and even more today with the advancement of technology people are much of our time pending from our Smartphone, Tablet, laptop and various electronic devices so necessary and entertaining to the time. These devices added to the usual distractions of the environment that occur at all times such as watching a person pass, suddenly hear a song, think of the following things or activities that we have to do, go with the thought to another place or any something else that distracts us, make us have the bad habit of using very little active listening, making it capture only part of the information and above all not getting to really understand the message that the other person wants to convey. We have said that active listening is to be able to really understand the message that we are receiving and for that, we must contemplate the following:

- Listen carefully to the words contained in the message that we are receiving.
- Identify the tone of voice used by the sender to transmit the message.
- Observe the body language (non-verbal language) used by the sender when transmitting the message.

If we can capture all those elements, we can say that we are really listening to the person who transmits the message.

When a message is transmitted, it is basically composed of 3 important aspects; the first one is the words. They come to be the content of the message that is used to give meaning to what we mean. It constitutes 7% of the communication that is transmitted. The second thing is the paralinguistic language. It becomes the tone or volume of the voice that is used to transmit the message. This constitutes 38% of the communication that is transmitted. Body language (also known as non-verbal language) is the third one. It comes to be the gestures of the face and body, the gestures and posture that a person uses when he transmits the message. This constitutes 55% of the communication that is transmitted.

These three elements are necessary to grasp them faithfully so that we can truly understand and understand the message we are receiving. Only in this way can we understand, apart from the same message that words are, the way the message is being transmitted. Listening to the tone of voice that is used (paralinguistic language) we can realize if the message is transmitted with joy, enthusiasm, apathy, sadness, concern, disinterest, etc. By observing the body language of the sender, we can realize their feelings, emotions or mood. Basically, by capturing the tone of voice and body language, we can realize if the message that is transmitted through the words is in agreement with what we see and hear.

A person can come and tell us, "I'm worried." That simple phrase can be interpreted in a different way. One way to do this is, if that phrase is heard with a low voice and the person's face shows anguish, stress, fear or uncertainty, then we can realize that he or she is really concerned about a particular fact. What he has told us (concern) is according to what he reflects. Another way to do this is if that phrase we hear in a normal tone of voice, and at the same time we see a smile or a relaxed attitude then we can realize that perhaps the person is not at all concerned.

As we see, although the content of the message (words) is the same, but gestures, attitudes, and everything non-verbal complement and helps define what we are listening. When we listen to a person say a sentence or a complete message we can get to really understand what he wants to say and how he feels or what he conveys by saying it. That is the only way to grasp a message faithfully, that is why it is the importance of putting aside all that we are doing or distracting us and can all our senses in the person who is talking to us. I think we would all like to be noticed when we talk or when we want the people around us to understand what we want to convey really.

> *"Honest communication is built on truth and integrity*
> *and upon respect for the one for the other."*
> - Benjamin E. Mays

Another important issue when communicating with people is the assumptions we use or handle frequently. Often we take something for granted or assume that a situation is true without having complete confirmation of it. We commit the error of not confirming it or not worrying to see if what we suppose is true. From there are born the famous "I was supposed," "I thought," "I imagined," that all they do is contribute to create uncertainty or not handle a good communication giving a fact. Interaction with people is an important day-to-day activity, and we cannot afford to guess things without first confirming it or making sure it is true. We think that other people think or grasp things just like us, or have been attentive to all points of a conversation, or have understood the message of an email that we have sent. It is common to hear phrases like "I thought you understood," "I assumed you knew the time of the meeting," "I imagined that you knew that the meeting point had been changed." And the worst of it is that we, we suppose, had not even given that information that we thought the other person knew. Many of the discussions or differences between people are born of miscommunication or assumptions. Many of the wars in the world are born as a consequence of not being able to communicate or interpret negatively some message that is received. It is essential to be able to confirm that the information that is transmitted can be received and understood.

Types of Massive Media

There are different mass media;

- **Magazines:** It is a periodical publication by notebooks, with writings on several materials or a particular. (Computing, mechanics, fashion, video games, artists, etc.)
- **Radio**: The transmission and reception of electromagnetic waves, where only words and music that can be included in advertising messages. The radio signal is heard in work or office locations as it accompanies to all kinds of people. Its varied programming and universal presence in receivers, allow the radio to be the medium closest to the people.
- **Television**: Instant transmission of images, such as photos or scenes fixed or in motion, by electronic means through transmission lines electrical or radio waves.
- **Internet:** Interconnection of computer networks that allows computers connected directly. The term usually refers to an interconnection in particular, of a planetary nature and open to connecting computer networks of official, educational and business organizations. There are also smaller network systems called Intranet, usually for use by an organization.

Elements of Success

Communication exists as an inherent process of human nature, as a process of transmitting information or a message in a given context and channel in which an issuer gives information through the code, which must be coded in a given medium to be received by a part of a receiver who should give feedback to the pattern. This process occurs throughout our lives, although in a specific way in organizations, is presented continuously and among all members of the same, plus the different ideologies and discrepancies of opinions is that there are problems in the mass, in addition to that there is no certainty that the orders given can be translated into the actions actually requested.

In the development of organizational communication, mention is made of the key concepts of communication, although there should be special emphasis on the barriers and constraints that may have arisen from the dynamics, hierarchy, and form in which organizations exist, as well as how the medium internal and external can affect it. It is important to mention that communication has a special application in the business field since it is central to the culture and organizational climate that have a significant influence on the specification of values and beliefs organizations that together help achieve the main objective that the organization pursues.

Distortion of the Context of Message and Semantics

The context and the semantics of the messages can represent a limitation when communicating since it can be understood in another way according to the concept, the message itself or the situation, although it also affects a lot if the issuing person has credibility or not.

Information Poorly Expressed

It appears when the one who emits the message to communicate, although to make it as clear and understandable as possible, use words that are not appropriate and are even incongruent by the terminology and structuring used, which implies high costs in the organization having to correcting the errors, so you must carefully take care of what will be said and if you can put a data table with role presentation so that the message is clear.

International Context Barriers

When there are restrictions derived from different ideologies, culture, language and different ways of action that make it complicated to transmit the message; such as translations, specialized concepts or different meanings from one culture to another.

Loss of Information Due To Limited Retention

It occurs when the information between individuals is not precise as it is given. In severe organizations, actions should be taken to support information, data replication and the use of multiple channels to communicate simultaneously.

Information with Limited Listening and Early Assessment

Since we do not all know how to listen, and when they are communicating, they avoid the speech circuit for the same reason, in addition to the hasty judgment of information, rushing and not analyzing the message.

Impersonal Communication

It is the use of means of communication that can restrict information between collaborators since it is not front with whom the message is transmitted, so it hinders trust, understanding and a correct feedback.

Distrust Or Fears In Communication

The relationship between the high hierarchy and the other levels ensures that the flow of communication can either improve or weaken, as well as a consequence of not taking care of the positive, trusting and favorable organizational climate and the work environment is tense and complicated by what there is uncertainty and alert so that communication is blocked.

Insufficient Time for Changes

Due to the information flows, significant and important organizational changes in the collaborators do not react in the same way, but it takes more than anticipated the adaptation and that delay generates problems in the communication throughout the organization.

Access Information

It is when the information and the flow of the same exceeds the magnitude and if understood it is restricted by what lends itself to doubt because of the mentality own beliefs and thoughts pro what is seen low priority to some important data for whom emits the message, or when there is excessive data can be given disagreements and errors when processing the message; which is why we must preside over the content of what is informed so that it is direct and understandable to avoid filters that detract from it.

Communication is an essential element that must exist in any company or organization so that it is correctly managed and can use communication as a tool for the correct transmission of objects, instructions, and processes to achieve organizational goals. It is necessary to pay attention in the way it is carried in the organizations. The reason for this is that some alteration in it or its processes can cause confusion, misunderstandings or erroneous orders that can mean errors that cost a lot to the organization. The reason why it is necessary for all those immersed in the organization to have a sensitivity to the codes, channels of communication to be able to encode information, for which they can use the various means of communication that can be formal, informal, direct, oral and written. These should arise from the collaborators at lower levels and also and mainly from those in senior management, where everyone should take care that this information to be communicated is given in the best way to avoid problems in the future. Likewise, the processes that are carried out for this purpose are auditable, this in order to improve.

""No matter what people tell you, words and ideas can change the world."
-Robin Williams

Proactive Passionate Popular Perceptive Precise

Polite Patient Peace Practical Planful Punctual

Principled Plucky Prudent Protective

Chapter 3

Are you an Influential Presenter!

*"A presentation with the direct participation of the Client
is worth more than a thousand images."*

The presentation of our company or our products is a theme that brings many people and companies to the forefront. I realize that in general, we do not know where to start, we make a mess while we present and we do not know how to bring the sale to closure. Presenting a product is an issue of crucial importance, because if we do not do it right the first time we do not have a second chance to try it. In this chapter, we will discuss some clues on how to do it right! Whether or not you are dedicated to the commercial function, it may be interesting for you if you want to improve your influence. Your calls and follow-up efforts have borne fruit, and now is the time to meet with the prospect in person and make your sales presentation. How do you make sure you're successful? Four elements could determine the success or failure of your sale:

1. **Understanding -** Put yourself on the same side of your prospectus.
2. **Need -** Determine the factors that will motivate your prospect to listen to you with the intent to buy.
3. **Importance -** The weight that the prospect destined to a product, profit, utility, price or temporality.
4. **Trust -** Your ability to project credibility, eliminate doubts and win the prospect's belief that the risk of purchase will be less than the benefit received.

Here is a closer look at each step so that you make every sales presentation a resounding success. To determine the information you need to "get into the person's time, which will lead to a sale." Your goal is to get the potential customer's attention and your willingness to have a committed conversation about how you can help with something specific, he says.

Before The Presentation

Know the Business of Your Customers

"Buyers are busy and inundated with information. Make sure that you are able to connect the value of your solution with that specific buyer, or he's not going to give you any time or your attention". As a salesperson, you need to know a lot about your buyer so you can address how valuable your product or service can be to him. Potential customers expect you to know their business, customers, and competition as well as you know your own product or service. Study your client's industry; knows its problems and trends and investigates who are their main competitors. Some research tools that you should have included the company's annual report, catalogues or newsletters, publications, directories of trade and internet instances.

Write Your Sales Presentation

A sales presentation is not something you do at the moment and without planning; you should always have it in writing. The basic structure of a presentation includes five key factors: a common point with the prospect, a business description, questions to understand the client's needs, a summary of your main selling advantages and a closing.

Make Sure You're Talking To The Right Person

This seems obvious, but many vendors forget it. Sometimes, after you release the entire sales presentation, the prospect tells you that it requires authorization from someone else. So, when scheduling the appointment, always ask if you are talking to the right person or if there are others involved in decision-making.

In The Customer's Office

Create Understanding

Before you start talking about business, create a bond with the customer. To do this, you must do your homework and find out what they have in common or if there is any recent news of the company. It is advisable to have an overview of both the company and the business to build an understanding between both parties.

Make Questions

Do not fall for your automatic sales pitch. The best way to sell is to ask the prospect some questions and direct the conversation. Your questions should be carefully selected in order to identify the prospect's needs so that you can point out how your offer can help you. It is advisable to ask questions that require "yes" or "no" answers. Ask questions that reveal the motivations of purchase, their problems or needs, and their decision-making process. Do not be afraid to ask them why they feel that way; that is how you will understand them.

Take Your Notes

Do not rely on your memory to remind you of what is important to a prospect. Ask her if it's okay to take notes during the meeting and write the key points. Make sure you write objections; so you can respond only to them and show the customer how will they get benefit from your product or service. These could be to save money, increase productivity, increase staff motivation or brand name recognition.

Learn To Listen

The salespeople who speak throughout the presentation not only bore the prospect but also end up losing the sale. A good rule is to listen to 70 percent of the time and speak only 30. Never interrupt; perhaps it is tempting to enter into the conversation to tell the prospect something you consider essential. But before you speak, ask yourself if it really is necessary for you to do it.

When you speak, focus on answering the questions. You can improve your listening skills by taking notes and looking at the body language of the prospect.

Respond With "Feel," "Felt" And "Found"

Do not argue when a prospect rejects you and tells you that he is not interested, has no time, or has already bought something like that. Just say something like *"Understand how you feel. Many of my clients had the same feeling. But, when they realized how much time they saved using my product, they were amazed.»* Then make an appointment; Prospects like to hear stories similar to theirs.

Deepens

If a prospect tells you *"We are looking to save costs and be more efficient,"* will you immediately tell him how your product will help you achieve it? A good seller would not do it; I would ask more to get to the bottom. You could say, *"I understand why it's important, and could you give me an example in specific?"* Asking for more information allows you to be in a better position to meet customer needs.

Find the Key Aspect

It usually happens when a customer has a list of needs, but usually, there is one aspect that motivates him to buy. The key to finding it is to recognize that it is something emotional and not something practical; a need for recognition, love or trust.

Suppose you are selling memberships for a sports club. For a prospect who will make a trip to the beach in two months, this aspect may be losing weight to look good in a swimsuit? For a prospect who recently discovered that he had high blood pressure, this could be to improve his health.

Eliminate Objections

When a prospect places an objection do not respond immediately. Rather, show empathy by saying "Let us explore your concerns." Ask for more details of the objections. Here are some strategies to do it:

- Offer An Option
  "Is it the delivery time or the financing that worries you?

- Get To The Heart Of The Matter
  "When you say that you want to think about it, what specific point is it that you should reflect?"

- Work On A Solution
  All sales must be a win-win deal. As you become more accustomed to making sales more familiar, you will be with objections. Make a list of them and propose some solutions.

Close the Sale

There is no magic to close a sale. If you followed the above steps, all you have to do now is wait for the client's order. However, some vendors make the mistake of not asking for the final decision. For some "close" sounds like something negative. If you are one of them, start by changing your thinking to something more positive like "decide". When I work in the development of commercial networks and practice the presentation of products to a new customer, I realize that we have ample space for improvement. The main issue that arises is how to order ideas consistently. In training and in sales we avoid language like I will teach you —rather we say let's explore together.

Many of us, when we talk, we do it with a clear objective "we have to sell." Sometimes you promote the action yourself to get clients with a presentation. At other times it is the organization that "invites" you to present a product or service before an audience to get sales. I believe that there will be more and more sales presentations. Customers are becoming more informed, but they need to get to know people - to create personal rapport - to make the decision. Moreover, the truth is that a presentation is an ideal occasion. That's why it's important - if your work revolves around sales - which you perfect your techniques in a context that helps you demonstrate your expertise to a potential client. Let me share with you today some necessary guidelines when applying sales techniques in a public presentation.

Keys to presenting a product or service in public.

Present Purpose

Although, it sounds obvious, many times we forget that the goal is to close a sale. Very often, in my formations, when I ask my students their goal they tell me things like "knowing the product." But, your sales manager would not be satisfied that many people know your product if no one bought it. If you do not have your destiny in mind, it is very easy to get lost along the way.

Create a Clear Structure

Make your talk easy for your client to follow. Not only will they remember it better, but you also will too. If your structure is simple, it is difficult for you to forget some key point, or to mix information that confuses the audience. Always notice that it's hard for people to remember more than three points. So carefully select the 3 points you would like your client to remember and place special emphasis on them when the end is near. Your structure should grow around those three strands and take advantage of the copywriting systems that marketing uses continuously.

Conversation with the Audience

Sellers often talk too much about themselves, their products or companies. They talk a lot, but they do not leave room for the problems or needs of the interlocutor. This leaves the audience out of the conversation. It eliminates the details of everything that you dominate and focuses the discourse on your potential client. Use questions and pauses to get involved in the speech gradually. They must feel that they are in the right place.

Memorable Stories

It's hard to remember cold information, yet we remember hundreds of stories just by listening to them once. When words become images and relate in time through characters, the assimilation by the audience is simple. The stories include intrigues, dialogues, humor, and tense situations... ultimately emotions. We are talking about using storytelling techniques to transform your data into something worth remembering.

Start and End With Strength

Keep insisting because it is essential to create impact how you start and how you end up. A loose start will make it difficult for you to connect with people, they will distract you. Moreover, a soft end will not help lead the action, rather invites people to leave because everything is over. Take time to prepare and memorize your first sentence and your final message. To give your product to know and get your business to grow, you have to develop a marketing strategy and familiarize yourself with different techniques such as newsletters and social networks.

That your marketing strategies are effective does not always mean that they are the right ones: Do you want to learn to show your product to your customers? One way to do this is to show it as a service. We are not talking about disguising your product or showing it as something that is not, but about changing how you talk about your company and how you relate to customers.

Increase Your Sales by Presenting Your Product as a Service

Why Marketing a Product as a Service?

> "Nothing is worse than a seller who does not stop talking about the advantages of your product or service. You can be successful in sales by engaging in a dialogue with the prospective buyer."

The products are visible and tangible, their purpose is clear and their benefits easy to evaluate. Services, on the other hand, bring more challenges to the marketing world. So why should you present your product as a service? Because you want your customers to see you as something much bigger than a simple assembly line. You want them to see you as an integral part of your life. Let's explore how you can practically implement these marketing strategies and understand their benefits:

Share Your Vision

Tell your users the story behind your company and your philosophy. Share with them how much your business helps you fulfil your aspirations. If you present your products in this way, they will go from being objects to dreams come true. By showing your passion and what motivated you to set up your business, you will make your customers part of the journey. Invite them to develop a deeper connection with your product!

Show The Human Side

One of the biggest advantages is that human beings realize the purpose of services, and this creates a relationship that products cannot imitate. But, products can be associated with a person. After all, they are produced and used by people. It's your job to emphasize how people are related to your product: it shows who your company is doing (like Wix we show you who we are) and interacts with your customers through social networks and newsletters.

Work With Testimonials

When real customers write reviews about your products, they will be telling you if they liked the product and if it served them. Nowadays, your clients have many ways to express their opinions, which means that a positive comment can be as beneficial to you as a paid advertisement. We recommend that you be proactive with testimonials and reviews, by inviting your past clients to share their experiences on different platforms. By showing that your customers' opinions matter to you. You also show that the relationship with your customers goes beyond the sale of the product.

Emphasize Long-Term Effects

Services-based businesses are looking for long-term results, whereas this does not always happen with products. To give a boost to your marketing strategy, you have to show that when buying your product, the customer will receive something much more important than immediate satisfaction. Find the right way to tell your potential customers how they will improve their lives if they use your product. How can you illustrate the long-term benefits of, say, a lamp? One direction you can take is to show how this lamp will get along nicely with the decor of the house. alt's not only functional but, it also has a nice design and the way in which it gives light will make the room look more inviting. You will be selling this atmosphere and relaxation. This will be your long-term effect.

Sell Experiences, No Products!

When you're promoting a product, you'll want people to see it as more than just a simple object. A Porsche, it is undoubtedly a beautiful object, but it represents much more than that: a luxury experience, refined style, and social status. "A pitch usually conjures up the image of a one-way presentation, with the salesperson talking to his prospect, which is not an effective way to sell," says Art Sobczak, president of BusinessByPhone. com. "The term is obsolete, and is often used derogatorily when talking about sales and sales personnel," he adds. Good marketing understands that when selling a product is not only selling the material but the experience that it entails. Consider all the positive experiences that your product can cause and let these be the ones who guide you when planning your marketing strategy. Great leaders succeed in inspiring and convincing their audience by starting the circle from the inside out by following the three steps we will explain below. And to explain them we will use the example of one of the leading companies in their sector - Apple - and one of its products star - the iPhone.

WHY?

Steve Jobs begins the presentation by talking about why his products. Apple is determined to change the world and revolutionize everything. Those are their values and shows them by taking as an example other products that they manufactured at the time, and that managed to change the rules of the game of their sector: the Macintosh and the iPod.

> "People do not buy what you do, buy the why you do it."
>
> - Sinek

Start the presentation by telling them why. In addition, the Why is an ideal element to use storytelling? The reasons why people do things are usually tied to their own personal history. Enjoy it! It tells the story that lies behind, and that ends in the Why?

HOW?

Once Jobs has already explained that is why *"is to revolutionize the world,"* explains how he intends to do it this time. Using a widescreen iPod touch screen, using a revolutionary mobile phone and an advanced internet communicator. Jobs explains how he aims to achieve his goal (his Why). List the Commas. These have all the sense of the world because the objective is already known. Probably, having started by explaining the Codes without first explaining why it would have been very difficult to understand, since, apparently, the three arguments seem to have little in common. So, once explained the why, explain the how to your audience.

WHAT?

The last step of the presentation of Jobs is talking about the product, the iPhone. At that point, people have already tuned in to Why Apple and have assimilated the why. Moreover, it only needs to materialize everything in a product: the what. The link that is created with the product is much stronger, because, above its characteristics, people value the motives and associated values. Starting the Golden Circle from within allows people to identify the Why easily and the How's in the product.

How to Present A Product And Love Your Customers?

The love of your customers is pure marketing, but in reality, this expression conveys something that we do want to do when presenting: captivate and seduce our potential client. So let's get to it:

First Phase: Philosophy

Once we have broken the ice with a customer, established the proper tuning, and started to get into flour, our mission will be to talk about the most philosophical part of our company and our products. That is, the whys, for what, the references, the values, the mission...

Imagine that we are selling energy efficiency solutions for industries, and in a meeting with the Director of Continuous Improvement of an organization we have to present a set of solutions that can help make your company more efficient. We could argue as follows:

"Maria, at Energy we believe that industries deserve energy solutions that reduce their emissions. Our mission is to achieve continued savings in energy consumption. This not only benefits you as an organization but also to society and how you know the entire planet. As you can imagine, today the best companies take their energy consumption very seriously, as well as their CO_2 emissions into the atmosphere."

This phrase, you can start by creating expectations in the other person, is your goal. One of the most effective tricks in the sale is not to talk too much so it would be time to ask a question such as *"How much of your company are you aware of with energy consumption?"* Then we would continue to argue and present the philosophy of our business.

"Among our values or way of working Mary we can highlight a total alignment with the needs of our clients, which means that we can work side by side with them to offer them better solutions every day. In the five years, we have been in the market, we have worked with clients. In addition, we also have a program of energy solutions for metal industries like yours, which represents a significant competitive advantage..."
Well, I will not continue, but you understand what I mean by "philosophy" right?

Moreover, we do it because in this phase the goal is to create expectations (without being too heavy making it clear).

Remember! The objective of the first phase is to create expectations, to arouse the customer's interest.

Second Phase: The Characteristics and Benefits

Once we have presented the customer in a generic way the company and the products, there will be a crucial phase in which we detect the needs of the same, we make him the protagonist of the meeting, we take care of what he needs most on our part, and later we present a solution. The solution will be presented by talking about the characteristics and benefits. Remember, there is no solution until the client has not been the protagonist of the meeting, he has told you what you need, what concerns you, and where exactly it stings. This is the main mistake of interplanetary commercial networks. In the second phase, we have a solution in mind, so it's time to present it. When we do this, we will emphasize using our best vocabulary and our best non-verbal language, as we are trying to influence the client to generate two key feelings: security and trust. Following our example would be something like this:

"Maria, within the program of solutions for industries like yours, we find two lines through which you can increase the energy efficiency of your company. The first of these has to do with the improvement of indicators in the production lines. In an industry such as yours in which there is a high energy consumption, most of that consumption comes from squirrel cage engines, such as I can see in almost every line, and can be improved by direct interventions on these and the different elements of the conveyors. Experience shows us that between 10 % and 20% of current consumption could be reduced..."

When we make this type of argument, we talk about the characteristics and benefits of our solutions. Always knowing what one thing is and what is the other.

- A micro-perforated seat is a feature of an office chair.
- Comfort at all times of the year is a benefit of this characteristic.

Returning to our example, if we wanted to say a characteristic and its corresponding benefit, it would be something like:

"Our interventions in production lines are very specific, and we make them point-to-point in line stop times. This means that from minute zero, you can see how your energy consumption decreases without hardly noticing that we are making improvements in the lines."

The Objective of the Second Phase Is To Convince
Third Phase: Concretion

Any product must be specified to reach the final agreement or close the sale. Without concretion, the client is left thinking about the product, but without elements of judgment to make decisions. In the concretion of the product, the solution must already be presented extensively, all its characteristics have been exposed, and then we will go to the stage of limiting all the terms to close the agreement.

This means that we will talk about:

- Approximate starting dates,
- Deadlines,
- Prices or investments to be made,
- Payment Methods,
- Guarantee
- Other specific conditions of the service provided.

If you analyze these three phases, you can realize that they make a lot of sense, since we go from the generic to the specific, and therefore, it is very difficult for the customer to turn against us when he does not know the details of the product or service presented. When you know them (in Phase 3) we are confident that we have done a great job of generating expectations and influencing him or her to tell us the definitive "Yes."

"If you go with the idea that they will only talk, talk, and talk and make the sale, it will be a battle almost lost. But, if you go with the idea that you will have a conversation and build a relationship with your prospect, you will have a better chance of winning."

Chapter 4

Negotiation into a Win-Win Long-Term Relationship

Introduction

"Everything is negotiable. Whether or not the negotiation is easy is another thing."
- Carrie Fisher

Negotiation has evolved over time and in business has become a science that we have to adopt all the Directors General as part of the success in our organizations. It is quite antiquated and out of context to negotiate the "old" and practices of "kicking" the counterpart, should (and I say MUST) be deprecated, as these intimidating tactics and "terrorism" are totally out of any winning culture. However, what happens to these bad habits of negotiating making use of the fear of the counterpart? ... It happens that until before the eighties, this was a common practice and the theory of Win-Loss was the custom because until that time Harvard and some other experts and universities still did not compile and reinvented the way to negotiate. Today the name of the game is called Win – Win. This method of negotiation of the late 70's and early 80's was created and compiled by the famous Harvard University and is not the "invention of the black thread" but a compilation of the best bargaining practices of various prestigious executives and, which, resulted in millionaire business and why not? Even billionaires.

The famous "tough" negotiator who was relentless, aggressive and even intimidating achieved "good" negotiations at first but made enemies and these partners, at the first opportunity, left the ship and left society without hesitation. That "soft" negotiator who granted every request (however absurd) of his counterpart was also common. As his insecurity and his eagerness to fall well make him fall into the game of becoming a "human carpet" and if it fell into the hands of a "hard" negotiator, he was sure to tear it to pieces. However, these styles of negotiation have remained in the past, and today the Win-Win negotiation has taken a preponderant role within the business realms.

The four steps to a Win-Win negotiation are: Build Mutual Trust, Be Transparent, Be Faithful and Be Fair and Equitable. I can bet that if you want to make a successful negotiation and present to the counterpart these four steps at the beginning of the negotiation, no one in your five senses will be able to resist, accept and guarantee the achievement of the goals set. That is a negotiation based on the long term, a negotiation with a broad vision, where what predominates are personal relationships, trust, synchrony of common goals and flexibility. Relationship-based negotiation seeks to create a long-term bond, where stakeholders will benefit and project themselves as partners, and strategic partners. A relationship where not only one goal and one goal, but several, where there is a projection of joint growth.

How Negotiations Work Without Losers

*"To make a win-win situation out of every deal, it takes a good
look at the negotiation and rhetorical feeling of the finger."*

A win-win situation should be the goal of any negotiation - whether with the colleague, partner or supervisor. For those who, according to the principle of "simply not surrendering" to an all-one-sided gain or unbalanced compromise, must face professional and private unpleasant side effects. Often, the "loser" is not only dissatisfied with the outcome but has come right before the head. In business days, this impression is often reflected in a tense working relationship and, in the worst case, leads to the customer or the supplier cancelling or changing supplier. If on the other hand, both negotiating partners are looking forward to the conclusion, their cooperation will be much more positive and constructive, not only in the short term but also in the long term, not least because a cooperative style of negotiation testifies to mutual respect and sympathy.

Cooperative Preparation

A deal, two winners - that would be the result of any negotiation. However, what is the ideal course of a negotiation talk - with such an ambitious goal in mind? How is it possible for all negotiating partners to make viable decisions and conclusions?

Quite simply: the win-win principle must already be reflected in the preparation. If for example, salary is negotiated, both sides should not only have their desires in mind. Ideally, the boss and co-workers have also taken into consideration the wishes, intentions, and goals of the other in advance and incorporated them into their arguments. Because: circles negotiation goal and justification for one party, a two-sided victory is excluded in advance. Both parties should, therefore, make themselves aware of their ideal result as well as the other, as well as the greatest possible compromise - both in their own and in the "foreign" camp.

The Visible Compromise

With a "cooperative" preparation, in any case, the cornerstone for a win-win situation has already been laid, and the doubly successful negotiation can go into the first round. Usually, the fronts are clarified first and foremost. Each party first presents its initial position in detail and puts its arguments into the field. These are the foundation for the subsequent opening offers.

In this case, the negotiation basis could look like the dealer offers a 10 percent discount, but the buyer requires 15 percent. The tender offer and counteroffer as in this case apart, phase two enters the negotiation: approaching over small concessions. Auto experts and prospective customers would now have to take a step towards each other in terms of price. It is important in this situation to make every "painful" millimetre, which one deviates from the desired goal, visible to the conversation partner, to signal to him: You have negotiated well, even if the meeting is really not easy. The danger that a compromise for both negotiators will feel like a loss business rather than after win-win is automatically pre-determined in this way.

Solution! For a win-win experience, counter-proposals should only be accepted "under pain" - with words or appropriate facial expressions. "I always sell you a car - even if you are a tough negotiator." This has nothing to do with acting, but with sincere feelings, because if we are honest: to make compromises almost hurt everyone. Moreover, only so does the other also get a feeling for his negotiation success. If possible: Please agree with pain.

The "Cake Enlargement Strategy"

Until now there is nothing to prevent a win-win situation. Only when the compromise is ripe out - without an agreement comes, she gets into the tipping. In the case of a salary negotiation, this would be the moment when the boss underbid the desired content with the words "This is my last offer" by a few hundred euros. Alternatively, the point at which the dealer cannot lower the price any further. Then the following is true: If the cake, which is haggard, is too small, it simply has to be enlarged. This is achieved with additional offers, which every negotiating partner with Win-win intentions should have in the hindquarters. Regarding an autocue, for example, there would be the offer to get three years of free customer service for the new car. In the case of the salary poker, additional leave would be conceivable or assets capable of acting.

Behind this cake-enlargement strategy is a simple psychological principle, which ensures the positive outcome of the negotiations for both sides. The so-called reciprocity or the law of reciprocity. According to this, anyone who sees himself in a negotiating position should also be able to win his opponent - no matter how big or small. Gifts do receive not only friendship but also mutual negotiation success. The reciprocity principle is the famous "How you like me, so you are" comparison. Or professionally speaking: the equity. If someone does something good, for example with a birthday card, then we are trying to compensate for our credit account by visiting this person soon. The result: Both parties feel themselves to be gifting or in a negotiation as the winner. Moreover, anyone who concedes a very good position is to reclaim something.

ZOPA : Zone Of Possible Agreement, BATNA : Best Alternative to a Negotiated Agreement.

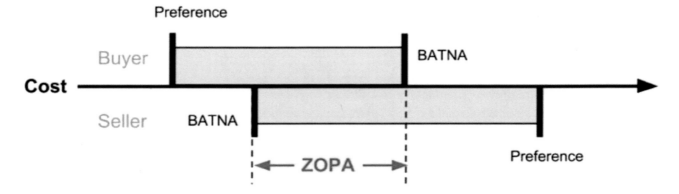

Figure 1: "Josh Brown "How To Negotiate Like A Pro: 5 Proven Approaches" 2017"

The Need of the Other

However, in order to implement this win-win strategy, there is an important prerequisite, because not every supplementary offer also makes the negotiation cake bigger. Only one offer, which is tailored to the needs of the other, makes a double victory from a negotiation. The reason: Often the demand of our counterpart is not at all equal to its actual interest. Behind the concern for more salary could in truth be the desire for more recognition or praise. It is therefore recommended to listen actively and to question the goals of the other person again and again. The true message is often found in the formulations. The beginning of sentences such as "I must insist on it ..." or "I hope ..." indicate where the focus is on the other.

In order to prevent misunderstandings, it is also advisable to summarize the content once again. With openings such as "In other words, you want ..." or "If I have understood you correctly, it is about you ..." one comes gradually closer to the core of the transaction. You can finally crack it - in the right place - with questions like "What do you mean?" Or the classic "Why." "As a result of the fact that the employee needs the money to be more mobile, a company car makes the negotiation cake so tasty that the deal is certainly sealed - without painful concessions and with two winners!

The Interests Decide

Too often negotiating positions are characterized by short-term negotiating goals or personal attitudes. This leads to win-lose negotiations, which are hardly ever reissued. Negotiations are a future-proof instrument. Both sides should ask themselves before the beginning of the negotiations how important the relationship with the partner is and what contribution the other side makes for their own well-being. If both sides are able to articulate their interests, viable solutions are created and not short-lived compromises with which no one is satisfied.

The Win-Win Situation

In a situation where the profit is obvious for both parties, there are usually also no differences. When a successful manufacturer wins a new sales opportunity, both sides have achieved a high added value. This also applies to a new project in which both partners can provide risk-minimizing assistance. Any good addition of one's own position by another is a win-win situation.

The Win-Win Evaluation

When the partners disclose their interests, an extension of the interests often occurs during the negotiation. Processes and achievements at the partner can be assessed and related to their own potential. This approach is also in line with the "enlargement of the cake" strategy, which can support the success of a negotiation.

The Win-Win Relationship

Negotiations based on the principle of win-win generally lead to a lasting relationship, which is characterized by a long-term value for both sides. The win-win principle is also worthwhile in negotiations whose success is not clearly foreseeable. For it gets the same rank for further negotiations, even if one side should achieve much more success.

The Characteristics of a Win-Win Negotiation

The basic principle of win-win negotiations is that the interests of personal sensitivities are considered separately and objectively. This makes the man "spared," and the communication can concentrate fully on the subjects of the transaction. A comparison of the values is also helpful. This is best achieved by clarifying at the beginning of the negotiation what the respective side feels as fair. This also provides a starting point for understanding the motives of the other side. This does not mean you have to accept them.

In order to be able to win-win negotiations, a high degree of communication competence is required. Also useful is the use of certain techniques such as brainstorming or trial ballooning.

When your business still has low revenues, negotiate in your favor to educate your employees, investors, and suppliers

After spending the hiring phase when it is still not possible to offer the salaries at the market level, inevitably, the employees and consultants will try to receive more money for work and will knock again at your door to reach a better deal. How should you handle this situation?

In principle, you must always respect the personal needs of your employees. This does not imply giving a raise every time you open, but it does require you to listen carefully to the reasons for requesting extra money. In many cases, they may not need an increase inflexibility of schedules, more vacations, training, more respect or inspiration. Most employees will not tell you the legitimate reason unless you ask for it.

When you are negotiating compensation, it is better to connect the employee to the performance of the company rather than linking it to the employee's performance during the initial stage. This not only encourages the company model to work - and thus pay everyone - but puts pressure on the members of each team to take responsibility for their performance, and that remuneration will be linked to the fulfillment of each.

The disadvantage of this incentive structure is that it could have a very capable employee who does not get a raise or bonus, due to the problems of execution among his colleagues. Therefore, we also suggest you review each of the situations and think about additional bonuses for exceptional performance. In practice, giving your employees a voucher for a trip or dinner with your family and friends may be better than a cash bonus as this can strain the other employees. In a small company that begins, a cash bonus that is divided among employees is a bad idea and undermines the levels of compensation that has negotiated with them.

With Investors: Clarity

A negotiation theory for start-ups requires a special approach. Here's how you can negotiate with investors when your business is in trouble.

Do Not Let Investors See You Worried

No one will invest a company if not even the entrepreneur is sure of the chances of success of his or her business. They may know that they have few initial funding options, but when they see success, they will temporarily forget the other options.

Write The Investment Conditions Before The Meeting

It will interact with venture capitalists familiar with the terms. It is essential to have clear investment conditions before you meet with them.

Make It Clear

Do not allow investors to restructure their investment terms unless they plan to conduct all fundraising. Most investors will want you to have clear policies; it is preferable that they concentrate on valuing the business proposal instead of the investment conditions. Avoid the temptation to negotiate individual terms with each investor, as you probably will have headaches to pay certain investors before others.

With Suppliers: Trust

During the initial stage, the problem of negotiating long-term deals with suppliers is recurrent. I recommend negotiating with suppliers in the same way as with investors: put your best face, and let them trust in your company. For example, let your suppliers dream about the day you will be their biggest customer. Negotiating favorable conditions will be easier when they perceive their company as a potential long-term customer rather than someone else. Suppliers and sales personnel of your company are more likely to accept an opportune price for a long-term contract with a cancellation proposal, rather than a small order and a short order. For example, if you are reasonably sure of your company's potential for growth, try to request the value of supplies for years, rather than for a year. But, be sure to extend the payments over the life of the contract and add an executable termination clause.

Learn To Trade In Your Favor Under A Win-Win Scheme

The art of negotiation is one of the topics most studied by business literature. Many books teach techniques to get the best deal possible for themselves. There are also concepts about finding results that are best for both parties: the so-called "win-win" negotiation.

The Concept of "Win-Win"

The "win-win" negotiation concept emerged at the Harvard Law School and dealt with cases in which the agreement reached cannot be better for the benefit of either party. By definition, the "win-win" negotiation is one in which no value was left aside, all creative options were analyzed, all available resources were placed to mutual benefit, and no one made unnecessary concessions to reach the desired result for both. The "win-win" negotiation is one in which the parties involved in a discussion obtain the best possible outcome for both.

Ask the Right Questions

When initiating a negotiation, we are likely to have only a vague notion of the interests and priorities of the other party. Many negotiators do not even ask the right questions to find out what is really at stake. In a win-win negotiation, it is important to determine whether our goals can connect with each other's ambitions. The more you know about what the other party expects, the easier it will be to negotiate if you know the interests of both.

Be Honest

What should I say about my goals and interests? In a win-win negotiation, it is essential that there be reciprocity. Therefore, you must be clear and realistic so that the other can better understand whom you are dealing with. In this way, you will establish a cooperative tone from the beginning, which will facilitate the dialogue. Obviously, you should not put all the cards on the table before hearing the other party, because there is always the risk that there is no cooperation on the other side. The idea is to do an "exchange of cards" and go play little by little.

Offers Alternatives

The best win-win agreements are often born after the parties have discussed multiple proposals rather than a single offer. The reason is that a single offer tends to produce an anchor effect and leads the discussion to an all-or-nothing situation. On the other hand, having more possibilities encourages both parties to communicate to find increasingly creative solutions for mutual benefit.

Third Party

To conclude, a good way to establish a win-win negotiation is to have a third element, neutral, that helps the parties to reach a favorable agreement for both. The third can also be an important piece to improve a preexisting agreement since it can present suggestions that neither of them had thought.

The third person can also help build a more confident environment by neutralizing the suspicion that one side wants to gain an advantage over the other. In this way, an environment conducive to the exchange of ideas is created. In addition, an outside opinion focused on the interest of both parties also helps to reduce the possibility of errors.

Knowing how to negotiate win-win is necessary to get what we want, but also to allow those who negotiate with us, also get what they need, as a basis for a long-term relationship. Negotiation is a procedure whereby two parties, each of which has something the other wants, agree to an exchange after a "haggling." So, if we want to access various resources to develop our project or venture, we need to negotiate. Moreover, "haggling" in a good way, knowing what the most that we are willing to give up and the least we are willing to accept is.

For example, if we need investment capital, commercial alliances, business contacts, good suppliers, etc. we have to negotiate in various facets that allow us to get what we want, giving in return what they want. Ex: We need money to launch our project, we must give equity capital.

Win-Win: If we want to establish lasting relationships, we must negotiate under the "win-win" premise. I win, but the other also wins. It is not advisable to play zero-sum, where I must win everything and lose the other. It is not a football match where you need to play to win. Here if the other feels that he lost, at some point, he will try to take the revenge.

Recommendations for Your Negotiations

Here are some simple and practical recommendations to keep in mind when negotiating:

- Before starting a negotiation, you have to plan your actions and inform
- This involves finding out what you want from us, what you need, and what valuable things I can bring you. That is our negotiating capital. Let us think how much it can "be worth" and if in return we can get what we need.
- Minimum, what do we expect from this negotiation? How far can I be willing to give in what they ask of me? Depending on the minimum I aspire.
- Think of different alternatives where we combine what we need with what we must give in return according to what we know our counterpart needs. Let's play with different tenor options.
- Being already at the "negotiating table," there are several points to take into account, which allow us to improve our negotiating capacity:
- **S**mile, invite relaxation, put aside you will look hostile or suspicious
- Know clearly how far we can go.
- There are several signs (e.g., crossed arms implies resistance, showing the palm communicates reliability, touching the nose implies something suspicious, etc.)
- Manage our times and possibilities
- In what is less important and protect what we are most interested in
- Occasionally, make it possible for third parties to mediate: When it is a complex negotiation or if we know in common a reliable third party.

When we are immersed in any negotiation process, all involved parties try to "pull the rope to their side" to get the best possible. However, "best possible" must be understood in terms of the totality of members, and not just those of a party. When in a negotiation one of the parties applies "selfishness," trying to get the best for himself, without considering the interests of the other party, it is possible that the negotiation does not advance, and even break. We must understand negotiation as a process of selection among the different alternatives, where a solution must be adopted that accommodates and is satisfactory for all parties involved. When we do this, we are in the "win-win " strategy, which maximizes efficiency for all and allows us to reach the best solution among all alternatives.

What Could We Do To Make Any Negotiation Easy, Quick And End Up Generating The Expected Result?

Before starting the negotiation, we must make an analysis that determines what it is that we intend to achieve. We define what we want, and what we do not want. Once we have identified this, we have very well delimited our "pitch." Next, we think of areas of satisfaction or interest for the opposing party. Thus, we prepare for negotiation, not only in terms of what we want but also considering what the other party wants or needs. When we have done this exercise, we will find an area of common interests. There, we will find one or several solutions that will accommodate the interests of all parties, and that is where we will find the way out of the negotiation.

When we have determined the common area, then we must choose between the best solutions for our interests. There we have already analyzed as a whole, and we have already considered the interests of others. Therefore, the solution that best accommodates our desire will be feasible and will continue to be an alternative based on the concept of win-win, where the interests of all parties are met. When you find yourself in any negotiation and notice that the opposing party is proposing a solution that solves your problem, but that does not attend in any way what you need or intend, it is time to remember that the negotiation must pick up a solution that will solve the interests of all parties (win-win). If this is not the case, any solution that goes through win-lose (win for one party and lose for the other) puts the negotiation at risk and could end up not advancing or even breaking the bargain. If we get to the point where the bargain is broken, we will find ourselves in the lose-lose scenario, where as a consequence of the lack of agreement, all parties could find themselves in a worse situation than they could achieve through the agreement.

After all, any negotiation involves several parties, and in no case can the criterion of one over others be imposed, for that would require no negotiation. The strongest part could end up imposing its will, without needing consensus with the others. At the moment in which there is negotiation is because there is something that must be decided by more than one person, and that is where we must think of the win-win as a negotiation strategy.

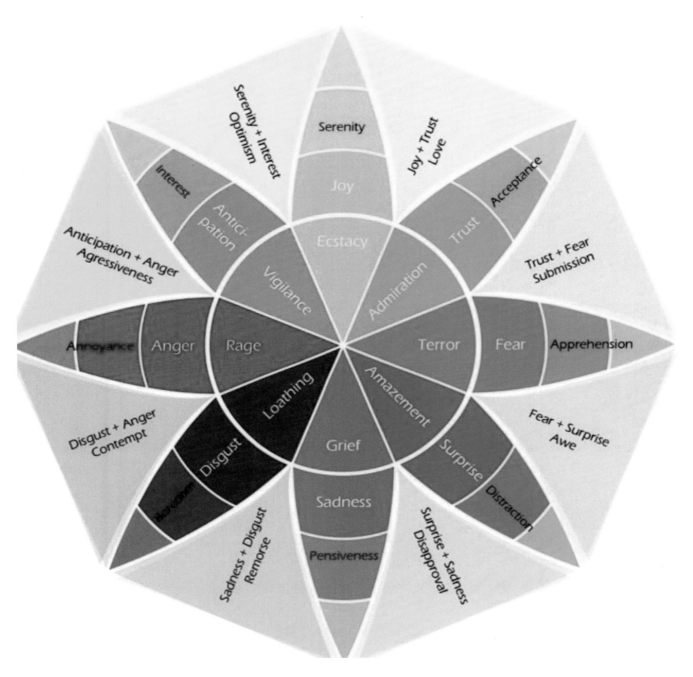

Figure 2: Plutchick. R. "The Nature of Emotions" American scientist 2001

Chapter 5

Emotional Intelligence Speaks About You

"No one cares how much you know until they know how much you care."
-Theodore Roosevelt

We have always heard that the IQ is a good indicator of whether a person will be successful in life. The intelligence test score, they said, could establish a strong relationship with academic performance and professional success. However, researchers and corporations began to detect decades ago that the skills and abilities needed to succeed in life were different, and these were not evaluable by any intelligence test. Emotional intelligence is the ability to identify, understand and manage emotions correctly, in a way that facilitates relationships with others, achieving goals and objectives, managing stress or overcoming obstacles. Whatever happens in your life, emotions, both positive and negative, are going to be there and can help you and make you happy or sink into an absolute pain, according to your ability to handle them. People with high emotional intelligence do not necessarily have less negative emotions, but when they do, they know how to handle them better.

They also have a greater capacity to identify them and to know what they are feeling exactly and also a high capacity to identify what others feel. By better identifying and understanding emotions, they are able to use them to relate better to others (empathy), to be more successful in their work, and to lead more satisfying lives. If we think carefully about the transcendence of our emotions in our daily life, we will quickly realize that there are many occasions when they influence our life decisively, even if we do not realize it. We might ask ourselves: Did I buy my car by calculating profitability and compared it with other models and brands? Did I choose my partner because I was objectively the best choice? Is my job the best salary? Most of our decisions are influenced to a greater or lesser extent by emotions.

Faced with this reality, it should be noted that there are people with a mastery of their emotional facet much more developed than others. Moreover, it is curious the low correlation between the classic Intelligence (more linked to the logical and analytical performance) and the Emotional Intelligence. Here we could illustrate this idea by bringing up the stereotype of student "nerd"; an intellectual machine capable of memorizing data and reaching the best logical solutions, but with an empty emotional and sentimental life. On the other hand, we find people whose intellectual abilities are very limited, but instead get a successful life when it comes to emotional level. This pair of extreme examples are unusual, but they serve to realize that more attention needs to be paid to this kind of emotional skills, which can mark our life and our happiness as much or more than our ability to score high on a test of conventional intelligence. For that, it is important to go deeper into Emotional Intelligence.

> *"The greatest ability in business is to get along with*
> *others and influence their actions."*
>
> - John Hancock

Many psychologists and human behavior experts believe that a person's emotional intelligence influences success more than his intellectual ability. There are many valid definitions of emotional intelligence. It is generally understood as a balance between quadrants: on one axis, "Person" and "Other," and on the other, "Understanding" and "Influence." Today many companies excel over technical skills, emotional skills. Empathy, self-control, balance... Emotional intelligence is one of the most sought-after skills in workers, which can be improved by following a set of guidelines. However, do you know how to recognize your emotional intelligence? If you want to become the perfect employee, read on.

This is how it should be in an entrepreneur who seeks to bring his idea to success:

Understand Yourself

Aristotle said that self-knowledge is the beginning of wisdom. It is true. To move forward, you have to be aware of what is going on in your head. Do you know what drives your emotions? If you are happy, annoyed, sad or angry, do you know the reason? It may sound easy, but for many people, it is not. To change your world, you have to start by discovering why you feel the way you do it.

Influences Yourself

This is your ability to modify your own behavior, as the case may be. It is the ability to be an enterprising person. Are you intrinsically motivated or need outside drive? Successful people are able to set personal goals, draw a plan to achieve their goals and execute this projection. Put simply; they are able to influence their own behavior in a positive way.

Understand Others

Understanding others is about empathy, your ability to understand what others are feeling and why, as well as knowing how your words and actions will be received by those around you. Without empathy, you could be driving people away without knowing why. It is very difficult to succeed if you do not understand others.

Influences Others

This is your ability to motivate people effectively. Your success and effectiveness are directly related to your ability to make people do what you want them to do. It is not manipulation because it is based on influencing others in a way that benefits you, but not to them. Motivating others correctly is always a win-win relationship. Successful people can influence others in a way that benefits everyone.

Does Emotional Intelligence Explain Business Success?

There are those who claim that prosperity is based on four factors: your intellect (how clever you are), your experience (including your education, previous work, and training), your effort and your emotional intelligence. Most organizations can measure the first factor very well through standardized tests, the resume talks about training and referrals serve to know how much a person strives. Although it is relatively easy to measure these paragraphs, modern companies can rarely measure the emotional intelligence of their employees. That is why they can get a job for which they were not prepared. However, this factor is vital to succeed, within a company or as an entrepreneur, because it balances the mind, thoughts, and spirit. It balances the person around you. Emotional intelligence is the most powerful tool for success, not only in romantic relationships but also in business. In fact, the same rules for achieving your goals in your company apply for love. Here are five practices that people with high emotional intelligence use to achieve success both at work and in their personal lives:

Follow Actions, Not Words

When I hire someone, I do not pay much attention to their sentences about accounting or hard work. Instead, I look for a solid track record to see if they deliver things on time, make calls, or close deals. In business and personal matters, talk is not worth it.

Analyze Yourself

We are all emotional beings, and sometimes small things can become big problems without need to be one. Intelligently emotional people know how to pause before creating a difficulty out of nothing. Did someone interrupt you at a meeting? Instead of complaining about that or planning your revenge, consider that person is distracted by personal issues in his home. Perhaps he felt himself being analyzed by his boss and is overcompensating with his noisy presentation. Get over it and give them the benefit of the doubt. It does not always have to do with you. The same rule applies to your love and business relationships. We all have bad days and flaws. Just because you are having a difficult time at work that you are already thinking of leaving. Take the incident as it is and move on.

Have The Final Goal Present

Those who succeeded in their lives and in business keep watch over what is important. This means letting go of insignificant things and potholes on the road that occurs every day. When you have the ultimate goal as a priority, it is easier to negotiate with a difficult client, to build successful partnerships, and to focus your energy on what is valuable without straying into small annoyances. That also applies to relationships. If a long-term relationship with your spouse is your priority, then you will not be bothered by things like leaving the toothpaste open. Even tougher issues such as money management or parenting are easier to negotiate when both are focused on a lifetime collaboration.

Get Rid Of Toxins

Good businesses feed on good energy. Negative people can destroy an organization. Entrepreneurs with high emotional intelligence know that there are enough positive people in the world who do not need to expend energy when dealing with toxins. Sometimes even high-performing employees are not a good choice if they are manipulative, combative or negative in the office. The same for your work and personal relationships. If someone steals your energy or makes you feel bad about yourself, have the strength to move forward. Emotionally intelligent people have little tolerance for those who are liars, critics, needy or have addictive habits. Some people are better out of your life or the other side of the room.

Stay Connected

Just because a relationship ends does not mean that you should destroy the bridge. Even if a deal falls, make an effort to take the heavy road and keep the connection alive. You never know when you will meet them again or if you will need them in the future. Just because a relationship does not last a lifetime, it means that they must move away from enemies. Very often relationships end up by certain differences or circumstances. When a bridge is available, there is a greater opportunity for you to enjoy better experiences at almost every level.

The Importance Of Emotional Intelligence

The most successful people in their lives are those with higher emotional intelligence, not necessarily those with higher IQs. This is because emotions, when not handled correctly, can end up destroying a person's life, preventing him from having satisfactory relationships, limiting his progress in work, etc. In general, emotional intelligence. It helps to succeed in all those areas of life that involve a relationship with others and favors the maintenance of more satisfactory relationships. It helps to maintain better health by being able to handle stress and negative emotions better like anxiety, without letting them affect them too much or for too long. Stress that is not handled correctly can negatively impact mental health, making you more vulnerable to anxiety and depression disorders. In addition, the person who does not handle their emotions well has many more emotional ups and downs and mood swings that damage their relationships and functioning. It helps to relate better to others. People with high emotional intelligence are better able to express what they feel to others and to understand what others feel. This allows them to communicate more effectively and create deeper relationships, both in their personal and professional lives.

> *"The factors that best discriminate, among a group of equally intelligent people who will show greater leadership, are not the IQ or the technical skills but those related to Emotional Intelligence."*

> - Daniel Goleman

Emotional intelligence is a quality that enables us to relate to ourselves and others. It covers the full range of relational possibilities we need to survive in an uncertain environment. Consequently, the greater the emotional intelligence, the better the relations with others, the others that are meaningful to us or simply acquaintances. In the emotional intelligence, three general components participate the subjective experience, the psychological reaction and the communication towards the outside. Moreover, in addition, several factors are specified that are part of the individual capacity to resolve the personal and relational conflicts so that the interactions with the others are full, healthy and satisfying.

To perceive and to interpret the own emotions and those of the others properly. The only way to properly manage emotions is to know how to identify what we feel so we can act on our decisions and not just react. On the other hand, the emotions of others are a source of information essential to know what they expect or need from us. Use thought to generate favorable emotions and moods. It is a circle of mutual influence: we think by interpreting what we feel and feel based on the thoughts we have. We can modify our thoughts so that we can avoid the discomfort generated by our negative emotions.

React appropriately to the stimuli. Two people, before the same stimulus, react differently, depending on how they interpret the meaning of that stimulus. For example, when someone makes an offensive remark, we can decide how we will react, whether calm or angry, responding or not to their provocation, based on the degree of emotional intelligence that we are able to put into practice.

When emotions overwhelm us, we lose our ability to respond to the message. The only thing we will remember later will be the feelings of hatred, betrayal or bad intention of the person with whom we communicate in a situation with little use of emotional intelligence. Either we will remember the guilt, the shame or the repentance for what we said, letting our disproportionate reactions lead us. Respect one's identity. The emotionally intelligent person interacts with others without ceasing to be herself; is able to express his opinions and feelings without hurting those of his neighbor. It is considered with the beliefs and the mood of the others and knows to be related without being neither submissive nor authoritarian.

"Emotions can get in the way or get you on the way."

- Mavis Mazhura

Emotional intelligence complements traditional intelligence. In other words, a person may not be very intellectual or academic, but he or she may be a person appreciated, loved and valued by his or her peers. This generates an attitude of appreciation to the people, which will lead him to be recognized for his emotional characteristics. A person with emotional intelligence will be a person who recognizes and manage their own emotions and the emotions of others. In other words, a person with emotional intelligence has a self-control of their emotions, produces motivation in themselves and in their environment, conveys tranquillity despite adversity, tolerates frustration and controls their own impulses.

EQ (Emotional intelligence) is very important for every leader as well as the employee. But, there have been some studies that gave results that how crucial EQ can be for the success of businesses, even trumping experience and IQ.

Center for Creative Leadership (CCL) in the USA in their research found that the deficiencies in emotional competence are involved in the executive derailment. 20,000 people and different organizations are served by Center for Creative Leadership (CCL) annually. This number also includes 80 companies out of 100 from Fortune. According to them, there are three main reasons for their failures which are the inability to work in a team, difficulty in handling the change and poor interpersonal skills.

Did you know that emotional intelligence represents 80% of a person's success, compared to 20% in which the IQ intervenes? Therefore, to use for the development of emotional intelligence phrases or famous inspirational quotes is a good resource to continue to advance and fulfil our objectives.

In this way, we will improve our EQ, understood as "a set of non-cognitive skills, abilities and competences that influence a person's ability to cope with the demands and pressures of the environment", according to Daniel Goleman, precursor of the application of intelligence emotional in the company and author of numerous works such as the successful ' Emotional Intelligence '.

And since we are talking about Goleman, let's start this collection of sentences with him: "True compassion does not mean just feeling the pain of another person, but being motivated to eliminate it."

Goleman and other experts in human behavior bring us the keys to improving our EQ.

"The great discovery of my generation is that human beings can change their lives by changing their mental attitudes,"
William James, founder of Functional Psychology.

"People with good frame of mind are better at inductive reasoning and creative problem solving,"
Peter Salovey, a psychologist who developed the concept of emotional intelligence after its introduction by Wayne Payne.

"Be aware that at this moment you are creating . You are creating your next moment based on what you feel and think. That's what's real,"
Doc Childre, founder of the HearthMath Institute.

"When consciousness is brought to emotion, power is brought into your life,"
Tara Meyer Robson, emotional coach and lecturer.

"The essential difference between emotions and reason is that emotion leads to action while reason leads to conclusions,"
Donald Calne, a Canadian neurologist.

Thus the painter **Vincent Van Gogh** said: *"Let us not forget that small emotions are the great captains of our lives and we obey them without realizing it."*

For his part, musician **John Mayer** stated that *"the intelligent person emotionally has skills in four areas: identifying emotions, using emotions, understanding emotions and regulating emotions ."*

Meanwhile, actor **David Caruso** left this eloquent quote: *"It is very important to understand that emotional intelligence is not the opposite of intelligence, it is not the triumph of the heart over the head, it is the intersection of both."*

Next to them, the American businessman **Alan Cohen** expressed the following quote: *"It uses the pain like a stone in your way, not like a zone for camping".*

"All learning has an emotional basis,"
Plato, Greek philosopher founder of The Academy.

"Trust, like art, never comes from having all the answers, but from being open to all questions,"
Earl Gray Stevens, a 19th-century American poet.

A Question Of Social Skills

Here's a list of the characteristics of emotional intelligence that will help you to know if you have or, on the contrary, you must begin to work it. First, we will look at personal skills. In this group, the most obvious emotional intelligence features are:

- **Self-Awareness**: recognize your emotions and effects; know your strengths and weaknesses; have the security of the value you have and your capabilities.
- **Self-Regulation**: self-control; maintain a line of honesty and integrity; assume responsibilities; be flexible in managing change; be open to new ideas.
- **Self-Motivation**: aim to improve or achieve a standard of excellence; assume the objectives of the organization; be willing to act when there is an opportunity; optimism and persistence.

In the field of social skills, emotional intelligence is manifested as follows:

- **Social Consciousness**: empathy; show an active interest in the concerns of others; anticipate, recognize and meet the needs of other people; develop and strengthen the skills of others; promoting diversity; read the group's emotional currents and power relations.
- **Social Skills**: influence, communication, leadership, the catalyst of change, conflict management, creation and relationships, collaboration and cooperation and teamwork.

> "Emotional intelligence is the ability to sense, understand, and effectively apply the power and acumen of emotions as a source of human energy, information, connection, and influence."
> - Robert K. Cooper, PhD

Emotional intelligence is characterized by having certain characteristics that converge in the following profile:

The Acquired Emotional Capacities

Emotional intelligence is a concept that comes from the hand of a new conception by which it is taken into account that intelligence is not purely and exclusively a matter of innate abilities but, on the contrary, the brain learns throughout the whole life of the person, and this will be mediated largely by emotional intelligence.

Recognition And Mastery Of Emotions

A person with this type of intelligence is able to recognize their own emotions and master them as well as being able to recognize the emotions of others and understand beyond what the words express.

Flexibility And Adaptability

People with a great capacity for emotional intelligence have the control of emotions and, therefore, present, in the face of the different daily challenges, a high flexibility and adaptability to the unforeseen changes. In other words, it was understood that not only was a high IQ sufficient, but the person was much more productive if he had a control of emotional intelligence since this generated much more adaptability and flexibility to the changes.

Empathy

Empathy is the ability to put yourself in the other person's place, to experience what the other person feels. In other words, empathy is to understand emotionally what happens to another person. However, a person with emotional intelligence has empathy but uses this ability to solve a particular situation. In other words, it not only understands the emotions of others and transforms them for the benefit of both.

Education Of Emotions

Several decades ago it was believed that emotions were not possible to educate them, nor even considered them. Today it is necessary and possible, according to emotional intelligence, to re-educate those harmful emotions (feelings of anger, anger, hatred, etc.) and transform them into positive feelings that help each person in their lives and about other people.

Solidarity With Others

A person with high emotional intelligence will have the feeling of solidarity about others. This concept not only includes economic or material issues but also involves solidarity from the emotional, the containment or the word that another person needs.

Assertiveness

A person with high emotional intelligence recognizes what he wants and knows how to achieve it because they have a balance between their emotions. That is to say, his emotions do not dominate him, but he uses the recognition of these for his benefit and that of others.

Leadership Skills

A person who considers these characteristics may be a leader for others because despite the difficulties a person with emotional intelligence is not overwhelmed by the challenges presented.

On the contrary, it seeks the solution, transmitting calm and serenity to the rest of the people. This is done not only from the word but also from the perception, communicating globally and directing a group of work, study, religious, etc.

Emotional Intelligence

Many things have been written regarding emotional intelligence. However, some guidelines can serve as examples, linked to these behaviors and ways to improve them. Here is a list of them:

- Personal experiences can be generalized to others, but only to a certain extent. The individuality of each must be understood.
- Think about the immediate reactions to the emotions, try to interpret them and learn from them.
- It is important to have people with whom you have the confidence to express in concrete form the emotions you feel.
- Avoid stimulants of certain sensations: usually, drugs, caffeine or different drugs can fulfil this role, which is contrary to emotional intelligence.
- The brain often undermines real emotions with others: people often get angry not to express sadness. To truly understand what emotion you feel is one of the highest points of emotional intelligence.
- Understand the role of emotions in the body, and not judge the fact of feeling bad or good as something more than they are: transient emotions.
- Valuing the triumphs of others, without that being permanently comparing and drawing conclusions for life itself.
- People with high emotional intelligence can accept mistakes and forgive them, but not with this by ceasing to learn from what they have done.
- Also, people should be able to identify their mistakes, not falling into a narcissism by which they think that everything they do well. It is about finding the balance.
- A space to enhance emotional intelligence in children is the game, and especially the sport. The exposure to losing that all participants have, makes those who end up winning can determine what those who lose clearly. This persists in the exercise of sport in the elderly, and even in situations such as job interviews.

"We define emotional intelligence as the subset of social intelligence that involves the ability to monitor one's own and others' feelings and emotions, to discriminate among them and to use this information to guide one's thinking and actions."
-Salovey and Mayer

A few years ago it was said that IQ tests have become obsolete since there are different types of intelligence. The intelligence emotional is a kind of related intelligence, as its name suggests, with emotions. However, within this, in turn, there are different types of emotional intelligence, and today we tell you what they are.

Types Of Emotional Intelligence According To Personality

According to several studies, emotional intelligence depends not only on emotions, but also on correct thinking, so it follows that the higher the IQ, the greater the development of emotional intelligence. Moreover, when we consider the five personality types with the highest emotional coefficient, it is observed that three of them had a high IQ and used to "think" more. It should be noted that the main difference between types of emotional intelligence is between men and women. On the one hand, women have more developed interpersonal skills, which means they are more aware of their feelings and others so that they can build better relationships. On the other hand, men have a greater sense of self and independence, which leads to higher self-esteem and greater ease in dealing with situations with high levels of stress. The truth is that emotional intelligence is a part of the psychology that is still taking its first steps because much remains to be discovered. However, it can greatly contribute to success, meet the certain job goals and improve personal relationships to feel good about yourself.

> *"You can conquer almost any fear if you will only make up your mind to do so. For remember, fear does not exist anywhere except in mind."*
>
> -Dale Carnegie

The managers, as well as the elements of the talents programs or human resources, progressively give more importance to the social skills and specifically to the emotional intelligence, empathy or control of the individual within the business or as a way to reach objectives that go more beyond purely economic or results.

So, in this new business culture that is expanding by all companies (large and small), we start talking about projects instead of jobs, employees or partners instead of employees and leaders, or managers instead of bosses. They are precisely those who are responsible for guiding the values of the company and identifying the talents and employees model to analyze later the contribution of individual value to a sum of total value that defines the company as a horizontal structure, that is, a system of collaboration between equals, and not as a mere hierarchical organization.

Emotional intelligence is used, in addition to the relationships and forms of work between employees and managers, also between the organization itself and the customers, where customer care plays a key role in business structure. It is in this department that the greater presence is being seen in today's companies, and the reason is very simple: customer relations have changed substantially, from a dominant position of the company towards consumers towards a system of relations you to you " in which the opinion, dissemination, and expansion of customer satisfaction can seriously hurt or, on the contrary, appear the company.

We have already seen some reasons why it is important to implement social values such as emotional intelligence both inside and outside the company, that is, between employees and the final relationship with the client. Now we will see the importance:

Generates A Climate Of General Trust In The Company

This causes a greater flow of communication, and the employees feel more comfortable and valued. This causes them to leave behind their consideration as a weak link, and to place themselves in a "win to win" relationship; the better the employee gets, the better he will go to the company. Motivation one of the tricks of emotional intelligence. If a collaborator is happier with his work, he will try to join efforts to achieve the objectives of the company, he will be loyal to this and will also try to keep his job so that productivity will grow. According to some studies, a motivated and happy employee is up to 2.5 times more productive than one who is not. Workers make their influence available to the firm for its growth.

Inter-Company And Intra-Firm Relationships Improve Substantially

It eliminates possible problems that may arise and limits the ability to work. In addition, it improves the communication and well-being of employees. These teams enjoy internal autonomy and are focused on the needs of customers, as well as improving the deal with this. The client, as we said before, becomes the epicenter of the process. That is to say, those who have leadership and talents that could not be defined without active human resources and talent management policy, where, in addition to the above, greater freedom and autonomy of the employee as well as the search and appearance of new values increasingly important as creativity.

In short, the guidance of employees gives results, trying to take the company as their own home, which causes them to put body and soul to improve all corners of organizations. On the other hand, it is the relations with the customers that define and evaluate the companies concerning the competitors, that the client stops being a weak member or with a model where it is the center and the most precious thing.

"To increase your effectiveness, make your emotions
subordinate to your commitments."

\- Brian Koslow

Chapter 6

Implications of Leadership

"If your actions inspire others to dream more, learn more,
do more and become more, you are a leader."
                                        - John Quincy Adams

There are as many definitions of leadership as there are people who have tried to define their concept. The lead management is the process of directing various work activities of members of a group or organization and directly influence them. The first is that leadership includes other people; to followers or employees. The members of the group or organization, given their own will to accept the orders of the leader of the leadership, help a lot to define the position of that leader and thus allow the process of leadership to pass pleasantly; if there were no personnel to command, the characteristics of leadership would be totally irrelevant. Second, it implies that leadership itself means a distinct distribution of power over the group's leaders. The members of the group are never without power; they can give shape to the diverse works of the group in different ways. In spite of this, the leader is always the one who has more power, as a rule. The third important quality of leadership is the ability to use different forms of power to influence employees' behavior in different ways. In fact, many leaders have directly influenced soldiers to kill, and other leaders have also influenced followers to make sacrifices of their own to benefit the company. The power that is acquired to influence leads us directly to the fourth aspect of leadership. The fourth and final aspect of leadership is combined with the previous three but stresses that on every occasion the leadership is always about values. The leader who overlooks the moral components of leadership will become transformed and acknowledged by others as something worse.

The leadership morality has certain values and always needs to provide sufficient information on the different alternatives to employees so that, when the time to respond to the proposal itself leadership of a leader, can choose with the intelligence that implies. It is important to note that although leadership very influential with administrative activities and leadership is very important for administrative activities, and the concept of leadership itself is not the same as that of management. The vast majority of organizations are underweight and over-managed, as Warren Bennis put it. An individual, perhaps an effective manager, good administrator, and planner, very organized and fair, but does not possess the sufficient skills that a leader must have to motivate. The kind of effective leadership that is needed in today's businesses is somewhat similar and somewhat different from what has been called "entrepreneurship." However, contrary to what happens with effective leaders, successful entrepreneurs are often very independent, tolerant, and very competitive people, and this is fine as long as they are just at the head of their independent businesses. Perhaps the reason some people cannot imagine a company in which dozens or hundreds of workers act as leaders is why their idea of leader matches what we have given to that type of entrepreneurs.

"The quality of a leader is reflected in the standards they set for themselves."
- Ray Kroc

It is a leadership that has a broad vision and has broad popular support. It is broad and general in a world that tends to focus on narrow and specialized. Others may be effective leaders in their ability to unleash enthusiasm and repayment, but lack the administrative skills to transmit the energy released by others. Faced with the constant challenge of dynamic engagement in our organizational days, a large number of them are beginning to appreciate managers who also possess leadership skills. The terms "leader" and "leadership," either because their use has not always been adequate to the reality they define, or because of the abuse and generalization that has been made of them, often lend themselves to confusion.

If we refer to Shaw (1976), leadership is "a process in which one member of the group exerts a positive influence over other members of the group." This definition, focused exclusively on the positivity of the leader, not only seems incomplete but also biased, because it would first be necessary to clarify exactly what is meant by "positive influence" and, on the other hand, to ask if the leader can also exercise - or in addition - a "negative influence" on the members of the group. Following Shaw, what he wants to express in his definition is that positivity should be understood as centered on the member of the group that holds the leadership, that is, on the leader, who, according to the author, exercises his guiding function not always in agreement with the objectives of the rest of the group.

The fact that the relationship between leadership and power is often extremely close contributes to highlighting this negative aspect; and is that, without a doubt, the leadership is based more often than not in some form of power. In this aspect, it is possible to emphasize, besides, the effect that can derive of a group in which underlies the basic assumption of attack-fugue. At this precise point, perhaps, we can ask a new question that expands the unfavorable connotations of leadership: Could the terms "negative" and "destructive" be paralleled? Personally, I choose an affirmative answer, but further radicalizing my opinion to the extent of extending such a paragon to the term "positive." The reason for the extension that I propose lies in the presumptions that will be presented below.

The fact that the leader's interests coincide with those of the other members of the group does not mean that they do not perceive reality subjectively and thus develop a form of thinking that confers internal coherence to their own mental models, from which it follows that what is perceived as positive may actually be the opposite and be unconsciously directed at the destruction of such a group. It may also happen that the aspirations of the small group are contrary to the goals of the society in which it is inserted. In this last aspect, while it is possible for an active and consistent minority to exert an effective influence over the majority, it seems rather remote, although the role that minorities may play in certain circumstances should not be underestimated.

Moreover, it is that the process of influence inherent in all forms of leadership - a process also linked to the exercise of power - moves on a continuum whose extremes are coercion on the one hand and persuasion on the other. Be that as it may, the conclusion to be drawn is that leadership is a function of the group; and which depends on the composition and characteristics of the latter, its defence mechanisms, the personal characteristics and mental models of its members, the leadership style of the leader, the relations of influence and the exercise of power, which connotations negative and / or positive factors inherent to this group function are manifested in one direction or another and with greater or lesser force.

The mechanisms implicit in this function and that determine the emergence of the leader have been explained from various theoretical approaches, each of which has contributed important contributions to the general body of knowledge. I subscribe, however, to Brown's (1988) statement that "The process by which the leader of a group is selected and the decision to adopt leadership or leadership is often mysterious." The underline of "often" is mine, and I emphasize it with the purpose of showing that I am making such a subscription because, since "frequently" there are no clear answers to the mentioned process, I have opted to avoid the theoretical explanations that, by innumerable and rich, would require an excessive space and time that does not justify the purpose of this work, but making it clear that in no way do I commune with the "mysterious" explanations, since these have no place in science.

Since Brown has mentioned leadership, and since leadership has become part of group social practice, especially from work, I will focus on this particular aspect of leadership in order to reflect about its possible advantages and disadvantages, and always in relation to what is exposed in the previous lines. Following Brown, co-leadership would seem to have potential benefits for group members derived from the fact that there are two people "with differentiated social characteristics who, in combination, can offer the group and each person more than they could offer separately." In this regard cites, among other aspects, the basic personal characteristics (age, sex, race, social extraction...); knowledge, experience, and ideas; the possible roles; the personality types that determine different managerial styles, etc. This variability would allow a greater possibility of adjustment of the characteristics of the leaders and the individual differences of each one of the members of the group.

Leadership would also have potential advantages for the leaders involved - leaders - as long as they meet certain conditions such as compatibility in terms of personality traits, ideas, goals, principles and values; and ability to establish a relationship based on affectivity and trust. The disadvantages, of course, would be given by the scarce possibility that the leaders could in principle assemble and maintain the necessary basic conditions of the considerate; and also by the difficulties inherent in a group whose dynamics of operation may be particularly complex. And it is precisely in the relations of influence and power proper to this dynamic, in the basic group assumptions and in the prevailing psychological mechanisms - in particular, the defence mechanisms - in which the leadership finds its greatest obstacles.

The members of the group will face attitudes of rivalry and competitiveness, authoritarian and irrational self-assertion, narcissism and sadomasochism, the tendency to impose the group's own objectives and use it to achieve them, as well as to manage the defence mechanisms developed by the group in the face of distress. In this context, a negative leader is likely to try to maintain group cohesion through the exercise of authority and therefore tends to autocracy to the detriment of shared direction and a system of constructive relations. On the contrary, a leader in positive truth would be attached to a democratic style and would favor the development of the potentialities of the group in the sense of progress.

It could be deduced from this that, as long as it is facilitated by a system of positive relations, and insofar as this system can only be developed and progressed within a democratic leadership style, it would be the ideal antidote against authoritarian methods and their consequences. Obviously, this is not entirely correct, or if it is a fvnon-condition of col- duration that co-leaders are compatible with personality traits, ideas, objectives, principles, and values; and demonstrate ability to establish a relationship based on affectivity and trust, these leaders are expected to act jointly and coordinately for both a positive and a negative project.

I think that both signs are not, in the subject of our study, antagonistic or mutually exclusive. As I have already stated in previous lines, positivity and negativity are aspects of the same phenomenon - as two sides of the same coin - that must be assumed in all their relativity and, ultimately, valued according to the implications and our particular interpretation of the same.

> *"A leader is one who knows the way, goes the way, and shows the way."*
> - John C. Maxwell

The leader must wear a suit known as leadership, which must be made with qualities essential to fulfilling his task of leadership, guidance, and influence, these qualities are known as leadership implications and are self-esteem, motivation, control, power, authority, and ethics. Each behavior and action that the leader executes is related to the degree of authority, power, control, ethics, motivation, and self-esteem that he exercises. Then you will know the different qualities that the person who exercises the leadership should have.

Self-Esteem

"Outstanding leaders go out of their way to boost the self-esteem of their personnel. If people believe in themselves, it is amazing what they can accomplish."

- Sam Walton

Self-esteem is the opinion and positive feelings that people have of themselves for everything they are, think and feel, that is, their thoughts, their self-image and the degree of well-being that they feel with them. The above is expressed in phrases as I am very good at this, I always achieve what I propose, this is very easy, I like the way I am, and so on. When someone expresses themselves in this way is said to have a high self-esteem. However, some people have negative thoughts and feelings about themselves, and this generates a low self-esteem.

What Is The Relationship Of Self-Esteem With Leadership And How It Is Exercised?

Some people wonder if self-recognition will be enough to lead a workgroup or if they will be able to perform successfully on that team. The answer is certainly affirmative, since the fact of knowing themselves forces them to identify the negative thoughts that lead them to have a low self-esteem and after reflecting on them will transform them into positive thoughts, which are transmitted to the members of the group under their charge and encourages them to make a greater effort to achieve the goals and feel good about themselves. Self-esteem is that every negative thought is replaced by a positive one, in this way the mind is programmed and the way of communicating with ourselves and with others is modified to obtain better results in our life. It is possible that the economy and labor situation as complicated as the insecurity that we undergo affect your self-esteem, but if you want to become a leader you must be positive, so try to relate to people who have initiative, intelligence, that expresses correctly, but above all you will have to convince yourself that you are unique and wonderful.

Motivation

"Ultimately, leadership is not about glorious crowning acts. It is about keeping your team focused on a goal and motivated to do their best to achieve it, especially

when the stakes are high, and the consequences matter. It is about laying the groundwork for others' success, and then standing back and letting them shine."
- Chris Hadfield

Motivating is moving, and driving action· Every leader is a motivator. It can understand why people act in a certain way, and skillfully manages the springs that drive people, that is, motivations, so it creates a commitment and maintains it and captures the team)s interest in the task. There are two groups of factors that influence motivation; the first group corresponds to economic and environmental factors such as business policy, working conditions, salary, insurance, prestige. Moreover, the second group corresponds to the motivational factors like opportunities for personal growth, professional progress, increased responsibilities, recognition for work that is well done, satisfaction. A leader who motivates his subordinates must be able to give them security and arouse enthusiasm based on the ideas and goals pursued by the organization, and encourage them and involve them in the tasks to be done, as well as in the projects by the undertaking.

The leader for the influence he exerts on his followers or his work team manages to motivate them according to a shared vision and that can be summarized in the following phrase of Rodolfo: the others want what the leader wants for that reason another The motivation that the leader can use is personal recognition, as a strategy to move his team towards the same end and to see the work as a personal embodiment, but at the same time the leader and the subordinate must make a personal analysis of what motivates or motivates them towards the goals that make them feel good.

In this way, the leader becomes a source of inspiration that succeeds in attracting subordinates, encourages them to seek new paths and with their experience leads them to discover alternatives that they did not see before, which allows people to expand their range of action and increase your skills. The motivational leader is the one who gets people to trust in themselves. Recapitulating, the motivation of the leader's mission is to make a person move from a negative attitude to a state in which he believes he can achieve what is proposed so that the individual immediately changes his behavior, his mood, his willingness to work.

Authority

"A leader must have the courage to act on an expert's advice."
– James Callaghan

Authority is conceived as the social function of achieving growth in a community and its members. Authority is credit and faith which, by its merit and fame, is given to a person or thing on a given subject. That is to say, that said person, in this case, the leader, is attributed the power to exercise authority over his subordinates. In every organization or work team, a leader is needed who exercises the authority to direct the efforts and resources to achieve the objectives, and this authority seeks the common good of all the members and the progress, that is, to fulfil the goals of the organization and with the expectations of team members or followers. The authority is expressed in the right to indicate guidelines on how to develop a particular activity, hoping that they will be met or obeyed to ensure that the activity, whatever it is, obtains the best results. For example, the authority that your parents exercise over you, in spite of the conflicts that may arise, seek your welfare. Authority is a legitimized power, for example, in the organization chart of a company or organization, it is noticed that usually orders are dictated by a person who occupies a hierarchical position superior to the rest.

Now that you know what authority is and the relevance it has in leadership, you know the various types of authority below.

Types Of Authority

- **Line Authority**: it is exercised by people whose activities contribute directly to the achievement of the organization's objectives, for example, managers, managers, etc.
- **Support Authority (Staff):** it is an authority to assist other members, who possess it assist, advise, recommend other members and facilitate the activities of the organization.
- **Functional Authority:** it is the one exercised by a manager on people from other departments, usually additional to the line authority that already owns.
- **Charismatic Authority:** it is based on the personal qualities of those who exercise authority. This is the leader's authority.

Power

"Power is not controlled at all--power is a strength, and giving that strength to others. A leader is not someone who forces others to make him stronger; a leader is someone willing to give his strength to others that they may have the strength to stand on their own."

- Beth Revis

The power is the degree to which leaders influence the behavior of others. The power will vary according to the prestige of the leader, that is, according to the degree to which others consider their actions to be significant, relevant or important. Leaders have power, and exercising leadership involves using it, but it is a conditional power that comes from their ability to help others succeed, and not to dominate or take action against their will. Power involves authority, control, and influence over others. Consider whether a person influences you right now, why? Moreover, why? It is likely to have some power over you, for example, your parents, your boss or a friend. There is a basic principle of power that states the following: a person has the power and ability to influence others because those others believe that it is in their best interest for that person to hold (hold) power. One way to lose power is not to respect employees or team members as this will fail to deliver positive results.

In organizations, different types of power are exercised, remember that a leader is not necessarily the manager or supervisor. The following are briefly detailed some ways of exercising power.

- **Reward Power.** It is a result of employees' belief that their leader will recognize that they have completed the various activities assigned to them.
- **Coercive Power.** Employees believe that a leader has the authority to impose punishments when they do not follow the instructions he gave them.
- **Legitimate Power.** When employees or supporters believe that a person›s position automatically gives them certain rights and authority.
- **Expert Power.** Others see in their leader a person who has knowledge, skills or specialized experience to achieve goals and objectives.
- **Reference Power.** It is based on the degree to which employees or followers identify with their leader and how they respect him or her.

Ethics

*"Ethics is knowing the difference between what you
have a right to do and what is right to do."*

- Potter Stewart

All leadership to function properly requires an ethic that signals the values that will govern their behavior and relationships with peers. Ethics refers to a set of values and norms that will be followed by agreement and knowledge. In addition to company policies, it is important that, as far as possible, employees become involved in agreements regarding standards.

An example of standards of this type is the following:

- Appreciate the work
- Speak well of the company
- Be responsible for the duties assigned to you
- Share information
- Trust administration
- Being part of the solution, not the problem

The ethical dimension is related to the notion of being and being. Having moral obligations guides us to conduct ourselves in an environment of recognition and respect for the human being in any field, whether at home, at school, in the community, at work or with society in general.

It is necessary that in the exercise of leadership the ethical dimension is taken into account as a fundamental element, and to keep in mind some considerations as to what the colleagues expect of me, how I should act with justice, how to express respect for my colleagues or subordinates, Is it important to act accordingly with what I think, that is, to be congruent? What is the positive and the negative for my colleagues, what values should we reinforce as a team, how to seek the benefit of colleagues, and so on. Leadership involves raising the team to a higher moral development where the company and society benefit by having people with a well-defined system of values and where integrity, honesty, and ethics are a characteristic of leaders.

Control

"Management is doing things right; leadership is doing the right things."
- Peter Drucker

The control is the set of means from which the leader ensures that each member in charge behaves responsibly and perform their tasks correctly, taking into account the expectations created and the consensus towards the objectives and goals that the group pursues. In order to exercise control, the leader relies on mechanisms through which he assures a certain behavior and commitment to his subordinates, for example, in companies it is common to find attendance lists, watch clocks or computers that track employee data from their fingerprint, all these devices record their time of entry and exit, thus maintaining a control over workers. The control in the context of organizations is an administrative function, is to measure the individual and organizational performance of the members, based on the goals and plans drawn and in order to ensure that they are met.

Supervision and follow-up should accompany control as an integral process, where the purpose is not only to control group members but also to detect possible deviations or problems from the objectives and thus help to correct them. Although control varies among leaders, they all have responsibility for executing it. The best way for the leader to make sure his followers do the tasks that are entrusted to them with skill and skill is to make sure they know what their maximum capacity is. In short, control involves monitoring the activities of team members and seeing each person do what he or she has to do.

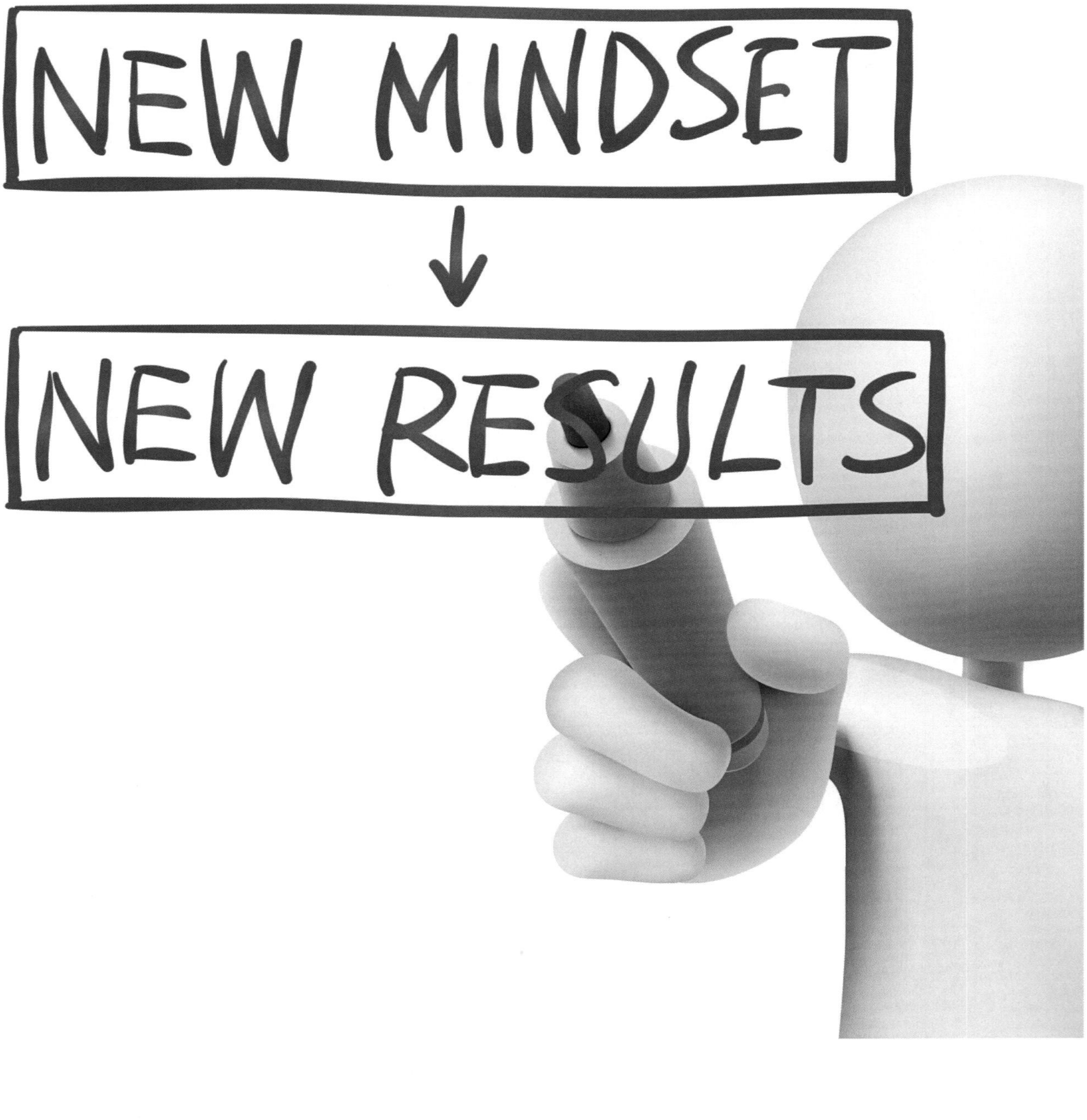
NEW MINDSET
NEW RESULTS

Chapter 7

You Become What You Think! Think Positive

*"The saying in business is that, 'You hire for skills and you fire for
behavior.' And one would argue that in order to move up in career,
to be promoted, to take on additional responsibility, in many ways
that's linked more to the attitudes and behaviors that you carry
rather than what you know technically about a given subject."*

- Gerald Chertavian

What can I do to buy my product? A simple answer does not exist, but good sales management can be an important support.

Your marketing department is responsible for lead generation in the sales process. Your sales management ideally works with marketing. So be sure to avoid friction points and focus on developing a fully-designed sales strategy.

Use Techniques Of Your Marketing

It is important to analyze the relationship between marketing and sales and to adapt to common goals. Exchange, and provide an identical set of data to help you examine your leads and plan further steps in your action. An essential step is the segmentation of leads. Concentrate on the buying probability of different lead segments and measure which individual steps your leads have gone through to buy your product or service ultimately. These steps may include various interactions with you personally, but also with your website, your newsletter or your social media appearances. In short, with your online content, such as e-book downloads, white papers, brochures, or visiting individual websites where you can see prices. So use the Sales Funnel as well as the appropriate tools and solutions of your marketing to measure the probability of your leads.

Why You Should Develop A Sales Plan?

A sales plan helps start-ups, but also all other companies, to work purposefully and resource-conserving and to manage the sales process sustainably. A well-designed sales plan accelerates the small steps in the sales process, creates new incentives and reduces the laziness of your customers. With a sales plan, you can not only optimize the sales process internally but also boost sales. If you are internally discussing a sales plan, you should also collect external information. Ask your customers where they have previously acquired products and services, which factors contributed to the purchase, and which argument convinced. The feedback from interested parties, which are still in the middle of the sales process and could not (yet) penetrate a purchase, can also be helpful. Ask for reasons for this delay. It may be due to a lack of decision-making authority or a missing building block in your service.

Creating A Sales Plan

Define comprehensible goals in your sales strategy. Finally, you need to convert your budget into concrete actions. Clear goals help you to make success measurable. In most cases, purchasing decisions are not rationally justified but are hit emotionally. Talk to your customers about the further development of the business relationship, the competition, and the project, and show how your product helps. Ask who is responsible for a purchase and who uses the product. Identify possible critics and search the conversation. If you are interested in soliciting other competitors or buying them, you should ask for their motivation.

When you have completed your sales plan, have it blessed. Get feedback from your peers and supervisors. Keep in mind that legal hurdles may be clarified or additional information must be attached to the sales plan.

Setting Up Your Sales Team

So how do you manage to create a sales team that will help you achieve your desired results? Look for good employees with the following characteristics and abilities:

- **Energy and Charisma**: Sellers convince not only by good arguments but also with their charisma and personality.
- **Patience:** Good sales staff listen and take time to their customers. So, when choosing your team, be aware of the competencies in relationship building.
- **Learning-readiness:** Learning-minded and capable employees never cease to expand their skills and learn new skills.
- **Goal definition:** With concrete goals, it works better and more motivated. You can expect new targets to be a new challenge for your employees.

- **Responsibility:** The best salespeople see the company's goals as their own - and assume responsibility.
- **Team competence:** The exchange with other members is particularly important to good employees. They do not keep new developments and discoveries for themselves but share them.
- **Self-Management**: Effective employees have developed their system, which allows them to synchronize time and effort.

Sales Management

Always learn about it and do not stand still. Deprecated methods do not always lead to success. Create new skills that are particularly valuable to your customers. As a sales manager, you must lead your team. Recall your colleagues to the shared goals. Focus on your leadership and motivation skills. Identify the strengths of each team member. Proceed strategically and bring out the best. Be always the first contact person for your sales team. In sales management, define short-term goals and celebrate with your team when goals are achieved. Develop effective sales processes that communicate your expectations to your team. Support your team by providing the right sales tools and IT solutions. Decide with your team which tools are ideal. Focus on creativity, constructiveness, and consistency in sales management. If you have these characteristics, you are almost certainly able to develop a sales strategy that will give you success. Be aware that marketing and sales are always mutually beneficial and mutually beneficial.Make sure that your sales strategy optimizes your processes continuously. A motivated, committed team is the guarantor of your sales success. Look for key competencies when selecting suitable team members. What are your successes so far? How is the willingness to acquire new knowledge and skills? Are your managers able to train, coach, and promote their personal development? Once you have established a good sales team, stick to your employees because these skills promise success and sales for your sales management.

"Investing in management means building communication systems, business processes, feedback, and routines that let you scale the business and team as efficiently as possible."

- Fred Wilson

Effective Communication

It is one that helps me to achieve my goals, focusing on what I want to communicate and staying in this goal. For effective communication, we rely on four qualities: rapport, empathy, active listening, and assertiveness. Firstly the rapport is to connect with the other person and try to understand the person with whom we communicate. This does not mean that we agree with the opinion of the other person, but we must understand the point of view of it. We must use a language and a style in the personalized conversation to the person before us, in this way this person will feel appreciated and will be in confidence allowing it to communicate clearly and without fears that allow a better communication.

We must also consider our empathy, is the ability to "put on the skin" of the other person. With this, we achieve a greater understanding of the person in his emotional plane, and in this way, we can synthesize his communication since our emotions can always distort it. If we can empathize, breaking the physical barriers, with feedback in the conversation, legitimizing the emotions of our interlocutor and avoiding moral judgments, we will create a bond of trust and connection that will affect our longed for effective communication. Another necessary quality is active listening; this quality consists in demonstrating to the interlocutor that his speech is to our liking, to get the other person to feel that he transmits his message to us. Everyone likes to feel listened to, and people admire what he speaks, so with this, we generate trust in the interlocutor. We managed to create a pleasant climate that would foster the fluency of the conversation and will help the other person to feel also listened to want to listen to us with the same intensity that we gave.

Moreover, the last thing is assertiveness. Assertiveness is the ability to say what you want or thinks not at the expense of others. Assertiveness is the perfect quality for aggressive or negative conversations, showing us how we can first keep calm in the conversation by lowering the tension and proving to the other person that we keep the dialogue open in a calm and conciliatory way. With these four qualities, we would have the pillars to get an effective communication. But, from my experience, if we want to achieve this missing goal the last point, an action that does not need any experience and that many times we forget... many times costs a smile and we despise the value it has, but the chalice that is achieved in a conversation with a smile on the face is totally different, until our voice changes when we talk with a smile.

Communication Skills For Team Management

All companies are work teams. From this principle, company directors must develop communication skills and adapt them to each case, because it never communicates in the same way even with the same resources. In addition, it is good to emphasize that never before had the management positions been so close to their collaborators. Until recently, managers were viewed from a distant, sometimes inaccessible perspective; now, thanks to the opening models, they have a direct and constant dialogue with their staff. This forces them to develop communication skills typical of the era in which we find ourselves, which is marked, as we have said, by a great flow of information. Let›s see what these skills consist of:

Active Listening

Managers must open not only new channels to communicate with their work teams, but also implement active listening; that is, to understand the message of the other person and give it the importance it deserves. The best indicator in this regard is feedback from the management.

Different Techniques, Different Situations

The manager of the XXI century no longer uses a single model of communication, because he knows that situations vary. Part of their job is to know what kind of message to use in each case and under what conditions. Alternatively, summarized in one word, versatility.

Non-Verbal Communication

In addition, it must be clear that communication takes place on two levels: verbal and non-verbal. Although the second is expressed implicitly, that does not mean that you pay less attention. On the contrary, signs, tone of voice, gestures, postures, and other elements are also part of the message that is transmitted.

Emotional Dominance

Managing groups is dealing with emotions of all kinds. One skill that all managers must develop is the emotional intelligence to get each type of message to find a moment, a place and an intention.

Clarity, Conciseness, And Creativity

With so much information that the companies handle, it is necessary that the managers be clear and as concise as possible. Long or overly elaborate messages tend to disperse and often lose the initial effect. To all this, we must add a dose of creativity, especially in situations where communication does not have the necessary fluency and must rely on some additional resource to achieve its goal.

Appropriate Channels

Finally, managers also must find appropriate channels for each message. If you know how to do it, you will almost guarantee the success of your communicative work. In conclusion, if we want an effective communication we only need four qualities for it and of course practice these qualities with a smile on our faces.

As conclusions can be said:

- You must know how to choose the right and optimal communication channel to transmit the information correctly.
- The concept of communication is always managed as a round-trip interaction, so it is important to know how to express and transmit the message correctly and at the same time know how to listen.
- In order to practice Active Listening, it is necessary to place all our senses in the person who transmits the message in order to faithfully grasp what comes to us and to understand their feelings, emotions, and mood.
- Words are a small part of the message we receive. More important is to be able to identify the tone of voice and body language of the person who transmits the message in order to understand the meaning of the message.
- It is important to eliminate assumptions whenever you can, to confirm that the other person knows the information.

"The strength of brand loyalty begins with how your product makes people feel."
- Jay Samit

Presenting your product or service is a key issue for any company that wants to sell and does business. The most important thing about a good presentation is to arouse interest and show that you are not like others, that you have something special, that your client or prospect has a problem that you can solve. According to Guy Kawasaki (one of the world's leading specialists in the field of new technologies and marketing), 95% of the presentations are ineffective, long and boring, with too many slides and poorly structured, with horrible animations and information overload; presentations that do not sell anything.

A sales presentation should be brief, simple and concise; your audience will retain a maximum of 3 to 4 messages per presentation, so take advantage of them to attack the customer's needs and earn their trust.

What To Do Before The Presentation?

- Make sure the purpose of your presentation is to convey your message memorably and to move to action.
- Whether the presentation is by you, a collaborator or a third party, it is necessary to summarize the main idea or theme in 15 keywords.
- Answer the question what do I want to cause with the presentation? You have to know what you want to happen as a result of someone seeing your presentation.

Steps To Prepare A Presentation

Short, Memorable, Blunt

Apply rule 10-20-30 when possible. Guy Kawasaki suggests that the presentations should not contain more than 10 slides, not to last more than 20 minutes and texts with 30-point lyrics. If in those 20 minutes and with 10 slides your presentation does not meet the expectations, surely you will lose. Simplicity should be your goal.

Be As Clear And Intentional

Answer the question what do I want to cause with the presentation?, what is the result that I expect when someone sees my presentation? Choose each word thinking about your client and the result, remove everything that is clear and intentional.

Incredibly Visual Slides

Avoid vignettes or bullets (very old-fashioned), instead, rely on pictures and pictures. Information is most effectively remembered when text and images combine. Remember: 93% of the message is transmitted visually. Please use good quality images and avoid Cliparts. Avoid excessive use of colors.

Hook Words

Use clear, simple and direct language, avoid complex, vague and confusing terms or words. Avoid technicalities that obscure and de-power presentations. Jack Welch once said, "Unsafe managers create complexity." Make sure that every word you insert creates trust and security. Use modern fonts in your words, avoid old type like Times Roman and never use Comics.

Memorable Moment

Establish an emotional connection with your client. Super important! You cannot miss in your presentation a moment that reminds the customer the benefit of contracting your product or service. Steve Jobs in each presentation created a memorable moment that neuroscientists call emotionally charged moment; this is the equivalent of a mental note that tells the brain Remember this!

Numbers And Statistics

Numbers contextualize, reflect and move to action. The larger the number, the more important are the analogies or comparisons they make.

Show The Benefits Of Your Product Or Service

May it always be a rule! Benefits and not Features, let them see what benefits customers will get if they buy from you, why they should buy from you, be sure to connect with their emotions through design, messages, and images. This can be caused by asking questions that lead to you're seeing your problem and how your product or service offers you a solution. Let it be clear that your business solves its problems by exchanging money.

Show The Sales Model

The purpose of this slide is to explain exactly what you are selling, what value you bring and what the price is. It reveals the magic of your product or service, what you offer to improve your business, productivity, life, etc.

Incite To The Purchase

Mention what are the following points in case of closing the deal. It mentions offers, deadlines, delivery process, response time, customer service, process and all details.

Order Your Presentation

Help your audience get the message in a structured way.

1. Introduction of the problem or need
2. Main cause or issue
3. Answer and solution
4. Net benefit and closing

Well used, any software will serve you, whether PowerPoint, Keynote, or some of the online tools available on the net. The important thing is to transmit your message memorably and effectively, for this you do not need a presentation this plagued with transition effects with many animations and endless text blocks on each slide. What matters is content, clarity, and minimalism are the best allies when preparing an effective presentation. The idea "less is more" perfectly sums up the philosophy that will guide you on the right path. Exploit the tool you use, put it at the service of your goals and do not let yourself be tempted by the default designs.

> *"Negotiation means getting the best of your opponent."*
>
> - Marvin Gaye

When you want to make a deal with a person, the ideal is that there is an agreement with benefits for both parties or also considered as the habit of win-win. Stephen Covey conveys this thinking to take into account that one person's success does not have to be the failure of another; in this way, you will maintain positive relationships. This is one of the six paradigms of human interaction, which also include the following: 'win-lose,' 'lose-win,' 'lose-lose,' 'win' and 'win-win or no deal '. However, we will focus on win-win by trying to find the solution for a common good and equity between people. To be able to achieve this, the characteristics or traits that must be expressed are of integrity and maturity to understand the needs of the other, which can be represented with the balance of objectives and benefits.

What Can We Do To Make The Win-Win Habit Come True?

By being clear about our objectives, we must achieve a balance between the other people being considered at the time of entering into the negotiation. Cooperation is a basic element that should be part of our personality and leave behind the feeling of wanting to compete. Generating options and alternatives will be a buying factor when making the cooperation so that it comes with harmony. In order to have a better knowledge and to be able to carry it out, we present the following interdependent dimensions of the win-win life;

- **Character:** Essential characteristics of integrity, maturity, and mentality of abundance.
- **Relationships:** Build and maintain relationships with the same thinking win-win.
- **Agreements:** The elements are of desired results, guidelines, resources, accountability and consequences that give definition and direction to what is wanted to achieve.
- **Systems:** It must provide sustenance in the organization where the reward of winning is equitable.
- **Processes:** It is recommended to contemplate the problem, to identify the issues, to determine the acceptable results and to identify new possible options to achieve the results.

If we feel good about the goals and the decisions that have been made to achieve the goals, then there will be a commitment to the action plan, not just for the other person but, for oneself. To all this, a bond of trust and respect will be generated so that when help is needed, you can turn to that person. We must think that many times we forget and not consider the option of mutual benefit, but that could be the best choice to achieve greater success. Remember that to be able to reach that end must be with the same intention of win-win.

> *"Sometimes when I consider the tremendous consequences of small things ... I am tempted to think ... that there are no small things."*
> -Bruce Barton.

There are many advantages offered by the use of negotiation for conflict resolution in educational management. Among them it is possible to mention the following:

- Satisfaction of the underlying interests of the parties to the conflict.
- Equity in the distribution of results.
- Identification of the options in order to select the best.

- Resolution of the conflict in a short time, clear, viable and lasting.
- Separation of people from the problem.
- Emphasizes integrative solutions. WIN-WIN
- Create a climate of openness and trust

Emotional intelligence is a concept that brings together various emotional abilities. These include empathy, sociability, communication, active listening, ability to delegate work, adaptation to change, creativity, among others.

Recognizing and managing these emotions is a differential advantage in the workplace. A person with these skills is able to achieve a good organizational climate and consolidate teams with these same capabilities. That way, you have creative workers, who enjoy looking for solutions, propose new projects, take the lead and feel confident. This is why Master's and MBA programs seek to motivate these characteristics in their students.'

These are the new requirements demanded by the managers of tomorrow's companies:

- **Technological Adaptation:** Leaders must be up to date with technological advances and open to future changes. They must be able to conduct the digital transformation of their companies in order to optimize resources and define new strategies for the competitiveness of their companies.
- **Globalized Vision:** In addition to mastering more than one global language for business, such as English, Spanish or Chinese, a manager has to have an international vision. It must also be sensitive to adapt its strategies to various cultural sensitivities, contact networks, and skills to develop business in a context of globalization.
- **Entrepreneur:** A manager must be an entrepreneur by vocation, with the capacity to reformulate business models and find opportunities. In his résumé, it must appear that he has put forward his idea of business on his account and not bound by the working circumstances.
- **Empathic, Resolute And Creative:** Empathy is vital for people management and global relationships. It also values the ability to make decisions quickly and solvency, as well as the creativity that is synonymous with innovation.

"A genuine leader is not a searcher for consensus but a molder of consensus."
                                                                        - Martin Luther King, Jr.

Leadership is a set of qualities and abilities that a person has with which is able to influence the way of acting or thinking of others, motivating them to make the tasks to be carried out by such people are performed efficiently helping in this way the achievement of both individual and team achievements. The charisma, knowledge, humility, and maturity of a leader can generate great benefits for the company, so it is important to have good leadership in management positions. These are some of the business benefits of having good leadership.

Motivation

Keeping the team motivated is a great effort to be made from leadership. A leader must be able to direct the individual efforts according to the qualities of each collaborator, is a talent that acquires listening to the others from the empathy and not from the critic; in this way it strengthens the advantages of each employee, thus achieving that individuals feel satisfied by their work and their achievements.

The motivational factor enhances the capabilities of each worker, encouraging them to achieve more.

Trust

Employees rely on leaders for their set of skills and values. A leader always greets and shakes hands with his colleagues, has a large repertoire of the various areas of the company and is willing to help and guide others, shares his knowledge and experience with humility, being in this way, his personality is usually grateful, and his support requested and grateful.

Culture of Work

Every company is discussed under certain values, principles, and goals, during the selection of personnel, usually seek qualified personnel, with certain technical or formal skills, but it is also very important that their values and principles be similar to those of the company itself. However, employees are likely to lose sight of these particularities and set them aside; however, a leader knows how always to relate and work under these principles; in addition, he knows how to make employees act under these same principles by making them notorious in operation of the company.

Enthusiasm

Leaders are enthusiastic about the new challenges, even though they believe they are difficult to achieve. Moreover, to adversities and changes, they know that they are not alone, they know that they have a competent team that supports it and vice versa, every employee has the leader as a guide to turn to in difficult times. All of them put their hands to the work individually and as a team animated to achieve in the best possible way each one of the projects. These are some of the great benefits of having good leadership within the company. Remember that born leader is very scarce, in general, leaders are trained as such, must learn to make proper use of their emotions, empathy and technical knowledge in a process.

Glossary

1. Accustomed: customary; usual. (Pg: 03)
2. Affinity (pg:11): a natural liking for and understanding of someone or something.
3. Borne: carried or transported by the thing specified. (Pg: 01)
4. Empathy: the ability to understand and share the feelings of another. (Pg: 03)
5. Enthusiastic (pg:02): having or showing intense and eager enjoyment, interest, or approval.
6. Erroneous: wrong; incorrect. (Pg: 08)
7. Fidelity (pg:02): faithfulness to a person, cause, or belief, demonstrated by continuing loyalty and support.
8. Haggling: dispute or bargain persistently, especially over the cost of something. (Pg:06)
9. Heterogeneity: the quality or state of being diverse in character or content. (Pg: 02)
10. Hierarchy: a system in which members of an organization or society are ranked according to relative status or authority. (Pg: 06)
11. Inevitably: as is certain to happen; unavoidably. (Pg:04)
12. Interlocutor (pg:02): a person who takes part in a dialogue or conversation.
13. Interlocutor: a person who takes part in a dialogue or conversation. (Pg: 04)
14. Interpretations: the action of explaining the meaning of something. (Pg: 02)
15. Intrigues: arouse the curiosity or interest of; fascinate. (Pg: 04)
16. Metaphors: a figure of speech in which a word or phrase is applied to an object or action to which it is not literally applicable. (Pg: 01)
17. Misinterpretations: the action of interpreting something wrongly. (Pg: 01)
18. Paralinguistic: relating to or denoting paralanguage or the non-lexical elements of communication by speech. (Pg: 05)
19. Predominates: be the strongest or main element; be greater in number or amount. (Pg:01)
20. Prestigious: inspiring respect and admiration; having high status. (Pg:01)
21. Protagonist: the leading character or one of the major characters in splay, film, novel, etc. (Pg: 07)
22. Psychotherapy (pg:12): the treatment of mental disorder by psychological rather than medical means.
23. Reciprocity: the practice of exchanging things with others for mutual benefit, especially privileges granted by one country or organization to another. (Pg:03)
24. Remuneration: money paid for work or a service. (Pg:04)
25. Undermines: lessen the effectiveness, power, or ability of, especially gradually or insidiously. (Pg:05)

Bibliography or References

1. Amy E. Boren (2010). Emotional Intelligence: The secret of successful entrepreneurship? Retrieved from http://digitalcommons.unl.edu/cgi/viewcontent.cgi?article=1054&context=aglecfacpub

2. David Goldwich (2010). WIN-WIN NEGOTIATIONS. Retrieved from http://nigc.ir/portal/File/ShowFile.aspx?ID=1d1adfef-fe5a-4bb7-a67f-405e57255abc

3. David Ly Khim (2017) 21 Habits to Become a More Effective Salesperson. Retrieved from https://blog.hubspot.com/sales/habits-to-become-a-more-effective-salesperson

4. Erika Andersen (2014), How To Be A Successful Salesperson - Especially If You Think You Can't. Retrieved from https://www.forbes.com/sites/erikaandersen/2014/03/03/how-to-be-a-successful-salesperson-especially-if-you-think-you-cant/#778346131fe8

5. Geoff Fitch (2009).Complexity and the Implications for Leadership Development. Retrieved from http://www.pacificintegral.com/docs/complexityld.pdf

6. Gocha Pachulia, Laura Henderson (2009). The relationship between Emotional Intelligence and Entrepreneurial Orientation. Retrieved from https://www.divaportal.org/smash/get/diva2:234296/FULLTEXT01.pdf

7. Greenberg, H.M., and J. Greenberg. (1983). The personality of a top salesperson". Nations Business. Retrieved from http://www.calipercanada.com/personality.htm

8. Iqbal N1 *, Anwar S2 and Haider N1 (2015). Effect of Leadership Style on Employee Performance Retrieved from https://www.omicsonline.org/open-access/effect-of-leadership-style-on-employee-performance-2223-5833-1000146.pdf

9. Jagdeep S. Chhokar,O. Jeff Harris, (1985). Implications of Leadership Theories for Management Development and Practice: Contemporary Perceptions. Retrieved from http://www.emeraldinsight.com/doi/abs/10.1108/eb027859

10. John C. Foltz (August 2011) Understand and Sharpen Your Decision-Making Skills. Retrieved from https://www.researchgate.net/publication/279192830_Understand_and_Sharpen_Your_Decision-Making_Skills

11. John Hamm (2006). The Five Messages Leaders Must Manage. Retrieved from https://hbr.org/2006/05/the-five-messages-leaders-must-manage

12. Levine, T. (2000). The Top 10 Ways to Know if You Are a Teller or a Seller. Retrieved from http://www.topten.org/public/AF/AF102.html

13. Neqabi S.1 MSc, Bahadori M. PhD(2012). The relationship between emotional intelligence and entrepreneurial behavior. Retrieved from https://militarymedj.ir/article-1-939-en.pdf

14. Rhett Power (2017). 7 Qualities of People with High Emotional Intelligence. Retrieved from https://www.success.com/article/7-qualities-of-people-with-high-emotional-intelligence

15. Rhett Power (2017). 13 Win Win Tactics in Negotiating. Retrieved from https://www. inc.com/rhett-power/13-win-win-tactics-in-negotiating.html

16. Sardar, A., and M.A. Patton (2002). What Makes a Great Salesperson?: Links between our Heritage and the Future. Retrieved from http://www.anzmac.org/ conference_archive/1999/Site/S/ Sardar.pdf

17. Scott Edinger (2013), Three Elements of Great Communication, According to Aristotle. Retrieved from https://hbr.org/2013/01/ three-elements-of-great-communication-according

18. Xerox (2017) Ten Tips for Effective Public Speaking, Sharpen your competitive edge. Retrieved from http://www.office.xerox.com/latest/XOGFL-45U.pdf

19. Zameena Mejia   (2017). What you can learn from self-made billionaire Elon Musk about emotional intelligence. Retrieved from https://www.cnbc.com/2017/08/29/ what-you-can-learn-from-elon-musk-about-emotional-intelligence.html.